Regional **Chinese** Cookbook

Regional Chinese Cookbook

Kenneth Lo

Hamlyn
London · New York · Sydney · Toronto

To all the admirable 'new China hands'
who have achieved mastery over the Chinese language,
and all westerners who
have found fascination in my country,
where life is still tough, but I hope
things will soon become easier for
everybody.

Other titles in this series:
Florence Greenberg's Jewish Cookbook
Complete Indian Cookbook by Michael Pandya

Photography by Paul Williams pages 25, 26-27, 46-47, 66-67, 86-87, 106-107,
125, 126-127, 145, 146-147, 166-167
Line illustrations by Shirley Touret

Published by
The Hamlyn Publishing Group Limited
London · New York · Sydney · Toronto
Astronaut House, Feltham, Middlesex, England
© Copyright The Hamlyn Publishing Group Limited 1981
Third impression 1983

ISBN 0 600 32238 6

Phototypeset by Computer Photoset Limited
Printed in Singapore

The regional maps at the beginning of each chapter are not in proportion to each other.
However, we hope they will give you an idea of the area from which your favourite dish originates.

Contents

Useful facts and figures

Notes on metrication

In this book quantities are given in metric and Imperial measures. Exact conversion from Imperial to metric measures does not usually give very convenient working quantities and so the metric measures have been rounded off into units of 25 grams. The table below shows the recommended equivalents.

Ounces	Approx g to nearest whole figure	Recommended conversion to nearest unit of 25
1	28	25
2	57	50
3	85	75
4	113	100
5	142	150
6	170	175
7	198	200
8	227	225
9	255	250
10	283	275
11	312	300
12	340	350
13	368	375
14	396	400
15	425	425
16 (1 lb)	454	450
17	482	475
18	510	500
19	539	550
20 ($1\frac{1}{4}$ lb)	567	575

Note: When converting quantities over 20 oz first add the appropriate figures in the centre column, then adjust to the nearest unit of 25. As a general guide, 1 kg (1000 g) equals 2.2 lb or about 2 lb 3 oz. This method of conversion gives good results in nearly all cases, although in certain pastry and cake recipes a more accurate conversion is necessary to produce a balanced recipe.

Liquid measures The millilitre has been used in this book and the following table gives a few examples.

Imperial	Approx ml to nearest whole figure	Recommended ml
$\frac{1}{4}$ pint	142	150 ml
$\frac{1}{2}$ pint	283	300 ml
$\frac{3}{4}$ pint	425	450 ml
1 pint	567	600 ml
$1\frac{1}{2}$ pints	851	900 ml
$1\frac{3}{4}$ pints	992	1000 ml (1 litre)

Spoon measures All spoon measures given in this book are level unless otherwise stated.

Can sizes At present, cans are marked with the exact (usually to the nearest whole number) metric equivalent of the Imperial weight of the contents, so we have followed this practice when giving can sizes.

Oven temperatures
The table below gives recommended equivalents.

	°C	°F	Gas Mark
Very cool	110	225	$\frac{1}{4}$
	120	250	$\frac{1}{2}$
Cool	140	275	1
	150	300	2
Moderate	160	325	3
	180	350	4
Moderately hot	190	375	5
	200	400	6
Hot	220	425	7
	230	450	8
Very hot	240	475	9

Notes for American and Australian users
In America the 8-oz measuring cup is used. In Australia metric measures are now used in conjunction with the standard 250-ml measuring cup. The Imperial pint, used in Britain and Australia, is 20 fl oz, while the American pint is 16 fl oz. It is important to remember that the Australian tablespoon differs from both the British and American tablespoons; the table below gives a comparison. The British standard tablespoon, which has been used throughout this book, holds 17.7 ml, the American 14.2 ml, and the Australian 20 ml. A teaspoon holds approximately 5 ml in all three countries.

British	American	Australian
1 teaspoon	1 teaspoon	1 teaspoon
1 tablespoon	1 tablespoon	1 tablespoon
2 tablespoons	3 tablespoons	2 tablespoons
$3\frac{1}{2}$ tablespoons	4 tablespoons	3 tablespoons
4 tablespoons	5 tablespoons	$3\frac{1}{2}$ tablespoons

NOTE: WHEN MAKING ANY OF THE RECIPES IN THIS BOOK, ONLY FOLLOW ONE SET OF MEASURES AS THEY ARE NOT INTERCHANGEABLE.

Introduction

With China now opening up rapidly to the West, whilst pressing vigorously ahead with her policy of 'Four Modernizations', the number of visitors and tourists from Europe and the Americas who travel to China each year is running into tens of thousands. Some have penetrated as deep into the country as Sinkiang and Tibet. Towns and cities which in the old days were little known to the 'old China hands', such as Yangchow, Taiyuan, Chengtu, Kweilin, Kunming, Nanchang, Changsha, Shengyang and Chanchung, have suddenly appeared on tourist maps during the past year or two. Whilst the 'old China hands' only hugged the treaty ports, the new generation of tourists are ranging far afield into the great interiors of China. In doing so, they have discovered for themselves the size and variety of China, and conveyed their experiences to those at home who had not yet had the opportunity to travel and wander so extensively. These discoveries seem to have greatly whetted the appetite of many people of western society, who have suddenly woken to the fact that there is more to Chinese food and cuisine than what they had eaten in the 'chopsuey' establishments throughout the western world, which during the past decade has become almost a part and parcel of the western diet.

This 'awakening' seems to have greatly increased the western interest in Chinese regional or provincial cooking. One of the purposes of this book is to provide some answers to this demand, by providing an illustrated bird's eye view of the principal areas of Chinese culinary practice and tradition, which have grown from the natural geographical divisions of this vast country over a long period of recorded history.

Before pushing you into the 'deep end' of Chinese regional cooking, (and I am a believer that the best way to learn anything new is to 'jump in at the deep end', mainly because one usually finds that it is less deep than one had thought), allow me to clarify and explain a little about the Chinese meal.

As a rule, there are a good many more dishes at a Chinese meal than at a corresponding western one. For example, an ordinary Chinese dinner at home usually consists of about four dishes, with one or two soups. The dishes are brought to the table at the same time, and the diners can help themselves as they please. At a dinner party, there may be ten or a dozen dishes (or more), served in courses one after another with an interval of a few minutes between each. One could well have two or three soups, two or three fish or seafood dishes, several mixed quick-fried dishes, as many stews, casseroles and poultry dishes, two or three meats, and several vegetables. This system gives an almost unlimited number of combinations when choosing and planning a Chinese menu.

The ordinary run of Chinese dishes are roughly divided into 'rice-accompanying' dishes (Fan Tsai) – plain home-cooked dishes; 'wine-accompanying' dishes (Chiu Tsai) – quick-fried, highly savoury, crispy-crunchy dishes (good for savouring between sips); and 'big dishes' (Ta Tsai) – the larger steamed casseroles and roasts.

At a Chinese dinner, which usually starts with some 'wine-accompanying' dishes, rice is often not served at all, or, it is used for the purpose of 'settling the stomach'. Rice is usually served with those dishes coming after the 'big dishes'. The soups simply act as punctuations between the courses. There is no precise rule for the choice of ingredients, but the different divisions provide a frame-work on which the variation of texture, taste, flavour and substance can be built. As soon as a westerner plunges into Chinese cooking, he or she will soon realize that we Chinese not only 'marry' a tremendous variety of ingredients, but we also use the techniques of 'multi-phase heating' and 'multi-phase flavouring'.

By 'multi-phase heating', I mean heating in stages: food can be steamed first and deep-fried afterwards; or, boiled first, simmered until almost dried, and quick-fried to a crescendo at the last moment before dishing out; or, deep-fried first and then quick-fried with other ingredients. As in chemical processes, the possible combinations of different types and stages of heating can be numerous.

In the matter of flavouring, this is also a 'combined operation'. For example, food can be marinated before cooking, after steaming, or between the first and second quick-frying stage. Here again, the possible combinations are innumerable.

When the food is plain-cooked, such as roasted, steamed, simmered or dipped or poached in boiling oil or broth, or barbecued over an open grill, the diners can usually choose among a wide range of both dry and liquid 'dips' and 'mixes' on the dining table, which give additional piquancy to the simply cooked food. The dipping of food into 'sauces' and 'mixes' on the dining table is a very important and integral part of Chinese food preparation and presentation.

Because Chinese cooking has resisted being turned into a precise science, there are no specific rules in the matter of timing, quantities, flavourings and heating. In many recipes, correction is often possible up to the moment when the dish is served. To talk to a Chinese chef about 'time' (seconds, minutes or hours) and 'quantities' (spoons, cups or pounds) is tantamount to talking to an artist about inches or the weight of paint used in the picture composition!

I have tried to choose recipes with ingredients which are readily obtainable abroad (occasionally one has to fall back on a substitute) because, basically, the most important thing in Chinese cooking is good fresh food of which there is plenty in the West, so there should be no difficulty in re-creating these dishes at home. However, there are a few basic ingredients and recipes with which one has to get acquainted before plunging into Chinese regional cooking – the glossary gives details of a few of them.

Let me not detain you a moment longer.

Peking

In Peking, as I remember it, the air seemed clearer, the sun shone brighter and the moonlit evenings were more crystalline than anywhere else in the world. In winter, the streets were filled with the aroma of roasting chestnuts. In summer, the jade-like willows, bent over by their own luxuriance, swept the surface of the innumerable ponds, lakes, moats and canals. Above all, there was a leisureliness about the life. There was time on golden afternoons to drink tea above the lake at the Summer Palace, and the people appeared more polite than anywhere else in China. All Chinese are sentimental about Peking, which they affectionately call *Ku Tu* (the Old Capital). Many westerners who have lived there have succumbed to its charm.

What of its food? Peking cuisine is, in short, the 'Top Table of Classical Chinese Culinary Art and the Metropolitan Cooking of China'. Yet, Imperial Kitchen and regional contributions apart, Peking cooking has only a limited range of dishes. It cannot, for a moment, be compared with the wide-ranging and enormous repertoires of Canton, Szechwan or East China. It seems to concentrate on mutton and lamb, for there are ample sheep in Mongolia, and on the locally bred ducks, large prawns (from the Gulf of Chihli) and river crabs which are so popular that there are restaurants which serve nothing else. With regard to vegetables, Peking cuisine appears to be preoccupied with the great white cabbage, which, in its many culinary uses, is a world of its own. Many of the Peking dishes are prepared with carrots, radishes, spinach and greens; and in the summer with tomatoes.

Methods of cooking here seem to be characterised by a drier form of frying, by barbecuing and by using raw materials in larger chunks. The hot cakes made from corn and wheat, and eaten with everything, are enormous; and the steamed dumplings are so solid that they fill you up in only two helpings. Garlic, ginger, onions, shallots and leeks are used plentifully. There is a good range of noodles, usually eaten boiled and topped with a mound of soy jam. Genuine native Peking food can be described as piquant and wholesome, but not the sort southerners would fall over backwards to eat unless they were converted.

In the famous East Market of Peking, there are dozens of intriguing 'small-eats' with a variety of local sweet and steamed dishes. But on considering Peking cuisine as a whole, one must take into account all the metropolitan dishes and the classical dishes handed down from the Imperial Kitchen. The range is then considerable and comparable with that of any other section of Chinese cooking. Indeed, some of the regional dishes which hailed originally from outlying provinces have achieved greater fame and recognition in the capital than they were ever credited with in their own native provinces.

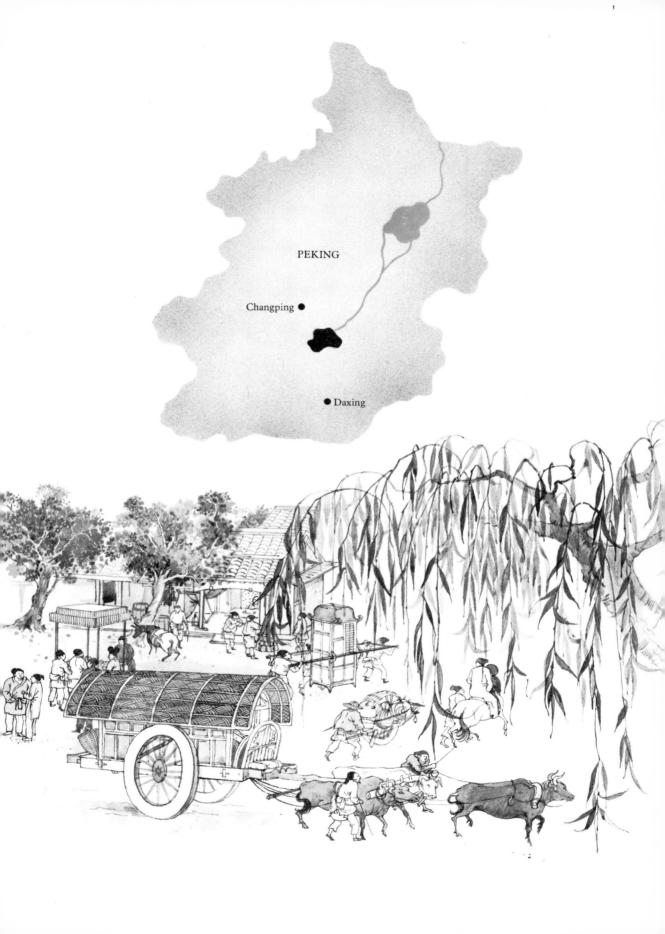

PEKING

Changping ●

● Daxing

Hot and sour soup

Suan La T'ang

This is a common Peking soup, easy to make and warming in the winter. Although chicken blood (solid form) and bean curd are usually included in the original recipe, they are dispensable. To be successful, the broth must be highly savoury before the hotness (pepper) and sourness (vinegar) are added.

Serve for a family meal

METRIC/IMPERIAL	AMERICAN
2 tablespoons cornflour	3 tablespoons cornstarch
4 tablespoons water	$\frac{1}{3}$ cup water
2 tablespoons soy sauce	3 tablespoons soy sauce
4 tablespoons vinegar	$\frac{1}{3}$ cup vinegar
$\frac{1}{2}$ teaspoon freshly ground black pepper	$\frac{1}{2}$ teaspoon freshly ground black pepper
25 g/1 oz bean curd (optional)	$\frac{1}{4}$ cup bean curd (optional)
1 egg	1 egg
2 dried Chinese mushrooms, soaked and drained	2 dried Chinese mushrooms, soaked and drained
25 g/1 oz breast of chicken	$\frac{1}{2}$ chicken breast
$1\frac{1}{2}$ teaspoons lard	$1\frac{1}{2}$ teaspoons lard
2 tablespoons chopped onion	3 tablespoons chopped onion
900 ml/$1\frac{1}{2}$ pints meat broth or consommé	$3\frac{3}{4}$ cups meat broth or consommé
1 teaspoon monosodium glutamate (optional)	1 teaspoon monosodium glutamate (optional)
1 teaspoon sesame oil	1 teaspoon sesame oil
$\frac{1}{2}$ teaspoon salt	$\frac{1}{2}$ teaspoon salt

Blend the cornflour with the water. Add the soy sauce, vinegar and pepper and mix them together. Cut the bean curd into 5-mm/$\frac{1}{4}$-inch squares. Crack the egg into a bowl and beat well with a fork. Cut the mushrooms and chicken flesh into matchstick-thin strips.

Heat the lard in a large frying pan. Add the onion and sauté for 2 minutes. Pour in the meat broth. Add the bean curd, mushrooms and chicken. Bring to the boil and simmer for 15 minutes. Add the cornflour mixture and monosodium glutamate. Stir the soup until it begins to thicken, then, as the soup is swirling around in the pan, stream in the beaten egg along the prongs of a fork. Pour it in steadily and slowly so that it separates into threads. Add the sesame oil and salt.

Give the soup an additional stir so that the 'egg-flower' (as it is called in China) will mix evenly with the rich brown soup. Pour into a heated tureen and serve immediately.

Tomato and beef broth

Hsi Hung Shih Niu Jou T'ang

This Chinese version of tomato soup is delicious if made as in this recipe.
The combination of meat, tomatoes and prolonged cooking produces a highly
tasty and satisfying soup.

Serve for a family meal

METRIC/IMPERIAL	AMERICAN
450 g/1 lb shin or stewing beef	1 lb stewing beef
450 g/1 lb tomatoes	1 lb tomatoes
1·4 litres/2½ pints water	6¼ cups water
1 teaspoon salt	1 teaspoon salt
1 teaspoon monosodium glutamate (optional)	1 teaspoon monosodium glutamate (optional)
freshly ground black pepper	freshly ground black pepper

Cut the beef into 2·5-cm/1-inch cubes. Place in a pan with boiling water
to cover and boil for 2 minutes. Drain. Cut the tomatoes into pieces. Place
the tomatoes and beef in a heavy saucepan and pour in the measured water.
  Bring the contents of the saucepan to the boil. Reduce the heat to as low
as possible (preferably placing the pan on an asbestos mat over the heat)
and simmer gently for 3½ hours. Add the salt, monosodium glutamate and
pepper to taste 5 minutes before serving. Pour into a large heated soup bowl
or tureen.

Crackling cream of fish soup

Yü Yung Pai Nai Keng

The Chinese use croûtons in their soup in the same manner as the French, except that the Chinese deep-fry their croûtons and place them at the bottom of the soup bowl, then pour in the soup. Because the croûtons are freshly deep-fried, they crackle when the soup is poured over them.

Serve for a family party

METRIC/IMPERIAL	AMERICAN
1 (100-g/4-oz) piece white fish (cod, bream, bass or sole)	1 ($\frac{1}{4}$-lb) piece white fish (cod, bass or sole)
600 ml/1 pint superior broth (see page 170)	2$\frac{1}{2}$ cups superior broth (see page 170)
1 tomato	1 tomato
1$\frac{1}{2}$ tablespoons cornflour	2 tablespoons cornstarch
300 ml/$\frac{1}{2}$ pint milk	1$\frac{1}{4}$ cups milk
1 teaspoon monosodium glutamate (optional)	1 teaspoon monosodium glutamate (optional)
1$\frac{1}{2}$ teaspoons chicken fat	1$\frac{1}{2}$ teaspoons chicken fat
1 teaspoon sesame oil	1 teaspoon sesame oil
25 g/1 oz dried Chinese mushrooms, soaked, drained and diced	1 cup dried Chinese mushrooms, soaked, drained and diced
25 g/1 oz green peas	$\frac{1}{4}$ cup green peas
1 tablespoon white wine	1 tablespoon white wine
1 teaspoon salt	1 teaspoon salt
vegetable oil for deep-frying	vegetable oil for deep-frying
50 g/2 oz bread cut into 5-mm/$\frac{1}{4}$-inch cubes	2 oz bread cut into $\frac{1}{4}$-inch cubes

Poach the fish in a quarter of the broth for 10 minutes. Drain, reserve the broth and discard the skin and bones of the fish. Mince the flesh to a fine paste. Scald the tomato in boiling water, peel, halve, remove the seeds and chop the flesh. Blend the cornflour with the milk and add the monosodium glutamate. Mix the chicken fat with the sesame oil.

Bring all the broth to the boil in a pan. Add the fish, tomato, mushrooms, peas, wine and salt. When it reboils, simmer for 1 minute. Stir in the cornflour mixture and the chicken fat mixture. Stir until slightly thickened.

Heat the oil to 180°C, 350°F, or until a day-old cube of bread turns golden in 1 minute. Deep-fry the bread cubes until golden. Place the 'red-hot' *croûtons* from the pan in a heated tureen. Bring it quickly to the table and pour over the soup. The diners should eat the soup while the *croûtons* crackle.

Sour and sweet Chinese cabbage

Ts'u Liu Pai Ts'ai

The people of Peking seem to like sour and sweet (rather than sweet and sour), with the emphasis on sour. This dish is a kind of Chinese sauerkraut, although it is a little more piquant.

Serve for a family meal

METRIC/IMPERIAL	AMERICAN
1 (1-1·5-kg/2-3-lb) Chinese cabbage (or a crinkly leaf type of Savoy cabbage)	1 (2-3 lb) Chinese cabbage (or a crinkly leaf type of Savoy cabbage)
1 tablespoon cornflour	1 tablespoon cornstarch
1 tablespoon water	1 tablespoon water
3 tablespoons vinegar	$\frac{1}{4}$ cup vinegar
1 tablespoon soy sauce	1 tablespoon soy sauce
1 tablespoon castor sugar	1 tablespoon sugar
1 tablespoon dry sherry	1 tablespoon dry sherry
2 dried chilli peppers	2 dried chili peppers
3 tablespoons vegetable oil	$\frac{1}{4}$ cup vegetable oil
1 teaspoon salt	1 teaspoon salt
3 tablespoons secondary broth (see page 163)	$\frac{1}{4}$ cup secondary broth (see page 163)
$\frac{1}{2}$ teaspoon monosodium glutamate (optional)	$\frac{1}{2}$ teaspoon monosodium glutamate (optional)

Remove and discard the coarse outer leaves of the cabbage. Cut away the base and cut the heart and inner leaves criss-cross into 3-cm/1$\frac{1}{2}$-inch lengths. In a bowl, mix the cornflour, water, vinegar, soy sauce, sugar and sherry.

Sauté the chilli peppers in the oil in a large frying pan for 1 minute. Discard the peppers. Add the cabbage and stir-fry over high heat for 3 minutes. Add the salt, broth and monosodium glutamate. Continue to stir-fry for 5 more minutes over medium heat. Add the cornflour mixture. Mix well with the cabbage. Stir-fry gently for 1 minute. Serve in a heated dish.

NOTE   Because of its sourness, this is a good dish to serve in conjunction with rich food, but because of its essential savouriness, it is also a good dish to serve with plain rice – hence its popularity with both the rich and the poor.

Red-braised Chinese cabbage

(Illustrated on page 25)

Hung Shao Pai Ts'ai

The memorable vegetable dishes in Peking seem to be the simple dishes of the common people – the type that they consume every day. This dish is one of them. It is interesting to note how the Chinese cook dried or pickled items together with the fresh ones to impart and compound flavour.

Serve for a family meal

METRIC/IMPERIAL	AMERICAN
1 large (1-1·5 kg/2-3-lb) Chinese celery cabbage (see page 157)	1 large (2-3-lb) Chinese celery cabbage (see page 157)
2 tablespoons soy sauce	3 tablespoons soy sauce
1 tablespoon dry sherry	1 tablespoon dry sherry
3 tablespoons superior broth (see page 170)	$\frac{1}{4}$ cup superior broth (see page 170)
1 tablespoon castor sugar	1 tablespoon sugar
4 dried Chinese mushrooms, soaked and drained	4 dried Chinese mushrooms, soaked and drained
3 tablespoons vegetable oil	$\frac{1}{4}$ cup vegetable oil
2 dried chilli peppers	2 dried chili peppers
1 tablespoon chopped spring onion	1 tablespoon chopped scallion
2 teaspoons cornflour	2 teaspoons cornstarch
1 teaspoon monosodium glutamate (optional)	1 teaspoon monosodium glutamate (optional)
2 tablespoons water	3 tablespoons water

Remove and discard the coarse outer leaves of the cabbage. Cut off and discard the base. Cut the inner leaves criss-cross into 3-cm/1½-inch pieces. Wash, drain and dry. Mix together the soy sauce, sherry, broth and sugar in a bowl. Finely slice the mushrooms.

Heat the oil in a large frying pan over medium heat. Sauté the chilli peppers and spring onion in it for 1½ minutes. Discard the peppers and spring onion. Add the cabbage and mushrooms and stir-fry over high heat for 4 minutes. Pour in the soy sauce mixture. Continue to stir-fry gently over medium heat for 1 minute, then simmer-fry for 10 minutes. Mix the cornflour with the monosodium glutamate and water. Add to the vegetables, turning the mixture over a few times. Serve in a deep vegetable dish.

NOTE Unlike a meat dish, which one tires of after continual eating, this vegetable dish can be eaten day after day.

Mongolian barbecued beef

K'ao Jou

Barbecued meat cooked in this manner was first introduced to Peking by visiting Mongolian dignitaries in 1644. It is still popular today.

Serve for a family party

METRIC/IMPERIAL	AMERICAN
1 (1·5-1·75-kg/3-4-lb) fillet or rump steak (100-225 g/4-8 oz for each serving)	1 (3-4-lb) tenderloin ($\frac{1}{4}$-$\frac{1}{2}$ lb for each serving)
225 g/8 oz small onions or 2 leeks	$\frac{1}{2}$ lb small onions or 2 leeks
Dips	*Dips*
eggs (1 for each serving)	eggs (1 for each serving)
soy sauce	soy sauce
ginger water (see page 160)	ginger water (see page 160)
chopped garlic in vinegar	chopped garlic in vinegar
tomato sauce	tomato sauce
dry sherry	dry sherry
sesame jam	sesame jam
chilli sauce	chili sauce
mustard	mustard
Plum sauce (see page 162)	Plum sauce (see page 162)
ground garlic in sugar	ground garlic in sugar

Hang the meat to dry for 5–6 hours. Then wrap it in foil and place in the refrigerator overnight. Remove any fat and gristle. Using a razor-sharp knife, cut the meat across the grain into paper-thin slices measuring about 10-13 cm/4-5 inches long and 5 cm/2 inches wide. Cut onions or leeks into paper-thin slices across the grain. The fine rings in each slice may then be loosened into 'onion wool' or 'leek wool'.

The cooking is done at the table by the diners. Traditionally, the fire-pot is thick metal measuring about 75 cm/30 inches across, covered with a thinly-meshed wire grill. The wire grill is rubbed with a little oil. When a drop of water sizzles, the grill will be hot enough to begin the barbecue. Place a dish of meat and two bowls (one empty and one containing an egg) in front of each diner. Ingredients for the dips are placed on the table. The diner breaks the egg into one bowl and beats it with his chopsticks. In the empty bowl, he blends his own dip from the ingredients listed above.

At a barbecue of this type, cooking and eating are simultaneous. Each diner picks up a little onion or leek 'wool' and puts it on the grill for $\frac{1}{2}$-1 minute. He selects a slice of beef, immerses it in his 'dip', then places it on top of his onion or leek to grill. He turns them over once or twice, and within $1\frac{1}{4}$ minutes they are cooked. He plunges them quickly into his bowl of beaten egg and eats them.

Deep-fried laminated fillet

Kuo T'ieh Li Chi

This is one of the 'laminated' dishes derived from the former Imperial Kitchen.

Serve for a banquet or family party

METRIC/IMPERIAL	AMERICAN
1 (225-g/8-oz) fillet of pork	1 ($\frac{1}{2}$-lb) pork tenderloin
$\frac{1}{2}$ teaspoon salt	$\frac{1}{2}$ teaspoon salt
1 tablespoon soy sauce	1 tablespoon soy sauce
1 tablespoon dry sherry	1 tablespoon dry sherry
$\frac{1}{2}$ teaspoon monosodium glutamate (optional)	$\frac{1}{2}$ teaspoon monosodium glutamate (optional)
1 tablespoon chopped shallot or spring onion	1 tablespoon chopped shallot or scallion
1 teaspoon chopped fresh root ginger	1 teaspoon chopped fresh ginger root
50 g/2 oz plain flour	$\frac{1}{2}$ cup all-purpose flour
1 egg	1 egg
2 tablespoons water	3 tablespoons water
100 g/4 oz pork fat	$\frac{1}{4}$ lb fat back
15 g/$\frac{1}{2}$ oz cornflour	2 tablespoons cornstarch
vegetable oil for deep-frying	vegetable oil for deep-frying
fresh parsley or chives to garnish	fresh parsley or chives to garnish

Cut the pork fillet into 5-mm/$\frac{1}{4}$-inch slices and marinate in the salt, soy sauce, sherry, monosodium glutamate, shallot or spring onion and ginger for 30 minutes. Blend together the flour, egg and half the water. Coat the pork fillet with this batter. Cut the pork fat into 10-15-cm/4-6-inch long, paper-thin slices. Place the coated pork fillet between sheets of pork fat to form a 'sandwich'. Press together on a board. Add the cornflour and the rest of the water to the batter and coat the 'sandwiches'. Deep-fry each 'sandwich' in oil over low heat for 4 minutes. Turn the heat to high and continue to cook for 3 more minutes, or until golden.

Chop each 'sandwich' into four pieces with single strokes without slicing backwards and forwards. Arrange on a dish and garnish with chopped parsley or chives. Serve with a dip containing a two-to-one ratio of salt to freshly ground black pepper.

Quick-fried
pig's kidney and sweetbreads
Ch'ao Yao Nao

This is a useful preliminary dish for a multi-course Chinese dinner.
Being highly savoury, it is a drinker's delight. The combination of kidneys
and sweetbreads provides a contrast in textures.

Serve for a banquet or family meal

METRIC/IMPERIAL	AMERICAN
350 g/12 oz pig's kidneys	¾ lb pork kidney
1½ tablespoons soy sauce	2 tablespoons soy sauce
100 g/4 oz pig's or other	¼ lb pork or other sweetbreads
sweetbreads	½ teaspoon salt
½ teaspoon salt	¼ cup bamboo shoots
25 g/1 oz bamboo shoots	1 small spring cabbage heart
1 small heart of spring greens	3 dried Chinese mushrooms, soaked
3 dried Chinese mushrooms, soaked	and drained
and drained	¼ cup chicken broth
3 tablespoons chicken broth	1½ teaspoons sugar
1½ teaspoons castor sugar	1 tablespoon cornstarch
1 tablespoon cornflour	1 tablespoon dry sherry
1 tablespoon dry sherry	½ teaspoon monosodium glutamate
½ teaspoon monosodium glutamate	(optional)
(optional)	1 clove garlic
1 clove garlic	3 tablespoons sesame oil
2 tablespoons sesame oil	2 tablespoons lard
25 g/1 oz lard	1 tablespoon chopped onion
1 tablespoon chopped onion	1 tablespoon chopped leek
1 tablespoon chopped leek	3 slices fresh ginger root
3 slices fresh root ginger	

Remove the skin and snip out the core from each kidney. Cut each kidney in half. Then cut each half lengthwise into six strips. On each strip, cut a dozen criss-cross slashes halfway through the strip. (These cuts speed and facilitate cooking.) Soak the pieces in fresh water for 10 minutes. Then drain and dry. Marinate for a few minutes in half the soy sauce.

Remove any blood vessels from the sweetbreads and blanch for 1-2 minutes in boiling water. Drain, sprinkle with the salt and set aside for 10 minutes. Drain and steam for 5-6 minutes and then chop into pea-sized pieces. Slice the bamboo shoots, heart of spring greens and mushrooms into thin slices. Mix the remaining soy sauce with the chicken broth, sugar, cornflour, sherry and monosodium glutamate. Crush the garlic.

Pour the sesame oil into a large frying pan. Swirl to coat inside with oil. Pour out the sesame oil and add the lard. When hot, add the bamboo shoots, spring greens, mushrooms, garlic, onion, leek and ginger. Stir-fry for 1 minute over high heat. Add the kidney pieces and fry for 1½ minutes over high heat, stirring all the time. Pour in the chicken broth mixture and add the sweetbreads. Stir-fry gently for 30 seconds. Serve immediately.

Red-cooked pork with carrots

Lo Po Shao Jou

Wu-Han is principally an industrial centre, and there is little wonder that the dishes produced here are more efficient than elaborate. This dish, if it had been prepared in an area or town of greater leisureliness, would probably take three times as long to cook!

Serve for a family meal

METRIC/IMPERIAL	AMERICAN
1 (675-g/1½-lb) belly of pork	1 (1½-lb) salt pork
225 g/8 oz carrots	½ lb carrots
20 g/¾ oz lard	2 tablespoons lard
600 ml/1 pint secondary broth (see page 163)	2½ cups secondary broth (see page 163)
2 cloves garlic	2 cloves garlic
2 tablespoons dry sherry	3 tablespoons dry sherry
2 tablespoons soy sauce	3 tablespoons soy sauce
1 tablespoon chopped onion	1 tablespoon chopped onion
1 tablespoon chopped leek	1 tablespoon chopped leek
½ teaspoon salt	½ teaspoon salt
3 slices fresh root ginger	3 slices fresh ginger root
1 teaspoon monosodium glutamate (optional)	1 teaspoon monosodium glutamate (optional)
1 tablespoon cornflour	1 tablespoon cornstarch
freshly ground black pepper	freshly ground black pepper

Chop the pork into 0·5 × 2·5 × 3-cm/¼ × 1 × 1½-inch pieces, discarding the skin. Cut the carrots, first in half, lengthwise, then zigzag across to obtain axehead-shaped pieces. Heat the lard in a saucepan and sauté the pork for 4 minutes over high heat. Add the carrots and broth. Bring to the boil and simmer for 5 minutes. Crush the garlic and add with the sherry, soy sauce, onion, leek, salt and ginger. Reboil and simmer for 10 minutes. Add the monosodium glutamate, cornflour blended with a little water, and pepper to taste. Bring to the boil and cook for 1 minute. Transfer to a heated dish and serve.

NOTE   Although this dish is cooked for only 20 minutes, the many in-gredients make it highly savoury and appetising. It is eaten with quantities of rice.

Stewed pork with sherry and ginger

Tun Chu Jou

This is the Chinese version of the 'eternal stew' – a great dish of the people! To enjoy Chinese stews and casseroles, one must learn to appreciate fat and skin; to the Chinese, they are savoury jellies.

Serve for a family meal

METRIC/IMPERIAL	AMERICAN
1 (900-g/2-lb) belly or leg of pork	1 (2-lb) salt pork or leg of pork
1½ tablespoons vegetable oil	2 tablespoons vegetable oil
900 ml/1½ pints water	3¾ cups water
2 tablespoons dry sherry	3 tablespoons dry sherry
2 tablespoons soy sauce	3 tablespoons soy sauce
1 tablespoon castor sugar	1 tablespoon sugar
1 teaspoon chopped fresh root ginger	1 teaspoon chopped fresh ginger root
1 tablespoon chopped shallot	1 tablespoon chopped shallot
1 tablespoon soy jam (optional)	1 tablespoon soy jam (optional)

Cut the meat into 2·5-3-cm/1-1½-inch cubes, preferably across the meat, fat and skin so that each piece will have all three. Heat the oil in a saucepan and sauté the meat for 4-5 minutes or until it has turned white. Meanwhile, boil the water. Add the sherry, soy sauce, sugar, ginger, shallot and soy jam, if used, to the saucepan and pour in the boiling water. Boil for 2 minutes and skim the surface. Lower the heat as far as it will go. Cover and simmer for 1½-1¾ hours. During the cooking, turn the meat over several times with a wooden spoon.

The meat and gravy should be served in a heated tureen or large bowl. Being rich, it is an excellent dish to go with a vast amount of rice. It makes a complete meal if accompanied by a dish of plain cooked vegetables.

Peking sliced lamb hot pot

(Illustrated on page 25)

Suan Yong Jou

*This method of cooking thinly-sliced lamb in a 'hot pot' at the table dates
from the reign of Emperor Shyanfeng of the Manchu Dynasty, mid 19th
Century, and has become one of the features of Peking. The most famous
restaurant for this 'do-it-yourself' sliced lamb hot pot is the Tung Lai Sh'un
in the East Market, where over 20 meat-slicing chefs are working full time.
A half-pound piece of meat usually yields 30 slices. The average slicing
speed of a specialist is 14 slices per minute!*

Serve for a family party

METRIC/IMPERIAL	AMERICAN
900 g/2 lb lamb	2 lb lamb (about 8 oz for each serving)
(about 225 g/8 oz for each serving)	1 (1-lb) Chinese celery cabbage (see page 157)
1 (450-g/1-lb) Chinese celery cabbage (see page 157)	$\frac{1}{4}$ lb spinach
100 g/4 oz spinach	$3\frac{3}{4}$ cups secondary broth (see page 163)
900 ml/1$\frac{1}{2}$ pints secondary broth (see page 163)	$3\frac{3}{4}$ cups chicken broth
900 ml/1$\frac{1}{2}$ pints chicken broth	$\frac{1}{4}$ lb transparent noodles
100 g/4 oz transparent noodles	*Dips*
Dips	soy sauce
soy sauce	sesame oil
sesame oil	sesame paste
sesame paste	vinegar
vinegar	chili sauce
chilli sauce	tomato sauce
tomato sauce	shrimp sauce
shrimp sauce	mustard
mustard	sugar and crushed garlic
sugar and crushed garlic	ground coriander
ground coriander	scallion
spring onion	

Cut the lamb into 18 × 5-cm/7 × 2$\frac{1}{2}$-inch paper-thin slices and allow about
15 pieces to each small plate. Shred the cabbage and cut away the thicker
stalks of the spinach.

Measure both the secondary broth and chicken broth into a 'hot pot' (see
note opposite) or a pan and place over the heat. As soon as the broth starts to
boil furiously, add about a quarter of the prepared vegetables and the
noodles. Within 1-2 minutes, it will reboil. This is when the diner introduces his own slices of meat, which should be immersed in the boiling
liquid with chopsticks. Meanwhile, the diner mixes his dip in the empty
bowl in front of him. The dip can be a mixture of some or all of the ingredients listed above. The diner can even have two bowls of different dips
for his own use.

The meat should be cooked for about 1 minute in the boiling broth. It should then be dipped in the 'mix' before eating. The vegetables and noodles help to provide a balanced meal. The remaining vegetables and noodles should be added to the hot pot as and when required.

NOTE   The attraction of this dish lies in the simplicity of materials, the freshness, due to instant cooking, and the effect of the quick piquant dip. This dish has yet to be introduced to the West; whoever introduces it should make a fortune!

The traditional Peking 'hot pot' differs from many southern 'hot pots' in that it is funnelled – the foods being cooked in the 'moat' which is approximately 13 cm/5 inches deep and 7·5-10 cm/3-4 inches wide. (At the Tung Lai Sh'un, the funnel is particularly squat in shape, measuring 15-20 cm/6-8 inches in diameter at the base and tapering to 7·5-10 cm/3-4 inches at the top.) The usual way to start such a burner is to place a few pieces of burning charcoal at the bottom of the funnel-furnace and then stack the funnel almost to the top with charcoal. After fanning the side opening at the bottom a few times, the smouldering should change into burning, and within 10 minutes there will be a beautiful blaze. The 'moat' outside should be filled with broth as soon as the first charcoal is introduced.

Any large, heavy pot or iron or steel casserole may be used for this dish, provided that it can withstand direct heat. It has to be large enough to contain at least 1·75 litres/3 pints (U.S. 7$\frac{1}{2}$ cups) of liquid together with the ingredients. The burner can be a methylated spirit, calor gas or electric type. The contents have to be kept at a rolling boil. The base for the 'hot pot' must be firm so that there will be no chance of the pot tipping over and spilling while the cooking is in progress.

With the aid of a fine gauge mechanical slicer and a chafing dish or fondue dish on the table, it should not be difficult to produce a western version of this 'hot pot'.

Sliced lamb
hot-scrambled-fried with onion

Chung Pao Yang-Rou

*This dish, from the Peking Municipal Public Service Bureau Catering
Department, is another favourite of the people which can be quickly
prepared. Yet, it is such a tasty and aromatic dish that, although it is
served in every dining hall and transport café, it is also found on top tables,
in elegant households or on party menus.*

Serve for a banquet or family meal

METRIC/IMPERIAL	AMERICAN
175 g/6 oz lean lamb, cut from the leg	6 oz lean lamb, cut from the leg
1 tablespoon cornflour	1 tablespoon cornstarch
50 g/2 oz spring onions or shallot	$\frac{1}{2}$ cup scallions or shallot
3 cloves garlic	3 cloves garlic
3 tablespoons oil	4 tablespoons oil
1 tablespoon soy sauce	1 tablespoon soy sauce
$\frac{1}{2}$ teaspoon salt	$\frac{1}{2}$ teaspoon salt
1 tablespoon sherry	1 tablespoon sherry
$\frac{1}{2}$ teaspoon monosodium glutamate (optional)	$\frac{1}{2}$ teaspoon monosodium glutamate (optional)
1 teaspoon sesame oil	1 teaspoon sesame oil

Cut the lamb across the grain in 5 × 2.5-cm/2 × 1-inch thin slices. Mix the
cornflour with 1 tablespoon water and in a bowl, mix thoroughly with the
meat. Cut the spring onions or shallots into 5-cm/2-inch segments, including
the green part and put aside. Crush the garlic.

  Heat 2 tablespoons of the oil in a large frying pan over medium heat and
stir-fry the lamb gently for 2 minutes. Remove the meat and put aside. Add
the remaining 1 tablespoon oil to the pan and fry the onion and crushed
garlic for 2 minutes. Return the meat to the pan and add the soy sauce, salt,
sherry and monosodium glutamate and scramble-fry over high heat for
1 minute. Add the sesame oil immediately before serving.

  Since this is a mixed, scrambled dish, no garnishing or decoration is
necessary. It should, however, be very neatly and carefully poured on to
a well-heated plain or decorated dish and eaten immediately. This is a
great dish for those who appreciate the aromatic qualities of quick-fried
garlic and onion.

Right *Red-braised Chinese cabbage (see page 16); Peking sliced lamb hot pot (see page 22).*
Overleaf *Peking duck (see page 32).*

Quick-fried sliced fish

Chua Ch'ao Yü P'ien

This is really a fairly simple way of cooking fish. The recipe is from the famous ex-Imperial chef, Wang Yü Shan. Many of the old Imperial chefs, now in their eighties, are employed by Peking restaurants.

Serve for a banquet or family meal

METRIC/IMPERIAL	AMERICAN
1 (225-g/8-oz) fish fillet (sea bass, rock cod, haddock or sole)	1 ($\frac{1}{2}$-lb) fish fillet (sea bass, rock cod, haddock or sole)
40 g/1½ oz cornflour	6 tablespoons cornstarch
600 ml/1 pint vegetable oil	2½ cups vegetable oil
Sauce	*Sauce*
1 tablespoon soy sauce	1 tablespoon soy sauce
1 tablespoon castor sugar	1 tablespoon sugar
1 tablespoon dry sherry	1 tablespoon dry sherry
2 teaspoons vinegar	2 teaspoons vinegar
½ teaspoon monosodium glutamate (optional)	½ teaspoon monosodium glutamate (optional)
2 teaspoons cornflour	2 teaspoons cornstarch
1 tablespoon water	1 tablespoon water
25 g/1 oz lard	2 tablespoons lard
1 tablespoon chopped shallot	1 tablespoon chopped shallot
1 teaspoon chopped fresh root ginger	1 teaspoon chopped fresh ginger root

Slice the fillet into $3 \times 1 \cdot 5 \times 0 \cdot 5$-cm/$1\frac{1}{2} \times \frac{3}{4} \times \frac{1}{4}$-inch strips. Coat in cornflour. Semi-deep-fry the pieces of fish in the vegetable oil in a large frying pan, adding each piece of fish separately (so that they can be handled gently and do not stick to each other). The frying should be gentle, over low to medium heat, and the fish should be removed after 2 minutes. Drain and set aside while preparing the sauce.

To make the sauce, mix together in a bowl the soy sauce, sugar, sherry, vinegar, monosodium glutamate and cornflour blended with the water. Stir and mix well. Pour off the oil in the pan and add the lard. When hot, add the shallot and ginger and fry for 30 seconds. Pour in the mixture from the bowl, and stir until the sauce thickens. Return the slices of fish to the pan. Turn them over in the sauce a few times and then transfer to a heated dish. Serve immediately.

Left *Ice-mountain fruit salad (see page 39).*

Royal concubine chicken

Hsiang Su Yu Chi

This is really the Chinese equivalent of coq-au-vin. *The most famous royal concubine (who was reputedly often intoxicated) was Yang Kuei Fei of the Tang Dynasty. Hence the dish is also known as Kuei Fei chicken. It is a very warming dish and, therefore, popular in the winter.*

Serve for a banquet or family meal

METRIC/IMPERIAL	AMERICAN
1 (1·5-kg/3-lb) chicken	1 (3-lb) chicken
2 tablespoons dry sherry	3 tablespoons dry sherry
2 tablespoons soy sauce	3 tablespoons soy sauce
6 spring onions	6 scallions
vegetable oil for deep-frying	vegetable oil for deep-frying
1·75 litres/3 pints chicken broth	7½ cups chicken broth
1 teaspoon monosodium glutamate (optional)	1 teaspoon monosodium glutamate (optional)
½ teaspoon salt	½ teaspoon salt
3 tablespoons red wine	¼ cup red wine

Rub the chicken inside and out with 2 teaspoons of the sherry and 1 tablespoon of the soy sauce. Chop the spring onions into segments 2·5 cm/1 inch long.

Heat the oil to 180°C, 350°F, or until a day-old cube of bread turns golden in 1 minute. Deep-fry the chicken in the hot oil for 7-8 minutes, or until it is just beginning to turn golden. Lift it out, drain and plunge into a pan of boiling water to remove most of the oil remaining on the surface. Place the chicken in a large flameproof dish or casserole and pour in the broth. Deep-fry the spring onions for 1 minute and add to the casserole, together with the remaining sherry, soy sauce, monosodium glutamate and salt. Cover and simmer over low heat for 2 hours. Add the wine and simmer for another 20-30 minutes. The dish should be served in a large heated tureen.

NOTE *Royal concubine chicken* is served halfway through a 10 or 12 course banquet, immediately after the quick-fried dishes. The chicken should be tender enough to take apart with a pair of chopsticks. The soup is marvellously tasty.

Aromatic and crispy chicken

Kuei Fei Chi

Sometimes in Chinese meals, one is surprised at the tenderness and crispiness of chicken which apparently seems only to have been fried. This recipe gives the secret.

Serve for a banquet

METRIC/IMPERIAL	AMERICAN
1 (1·5-kg/3-lb) chicken	1 (3-lb) chicken)
1½ teaspoons salt	1½ teaspoons salt
½ teaspoon five-spice powder (see page 160)	½ teaspoon five-spice powder (see page 160)
1 tablespoon chopped dried tangerine peel (see page 159)	1 tablespoon chopped dried tangerine peel (see page 159)
1 tablespoon chopped onion	1 tablespoon chopped onion
1 teaspoon chopped fresh root ginger	1 teaspoon chopped fresh ginger root
2 tablespoons soy sauce	3 tablespoons soy sauce
1½ teaspoons castor sugar	1½ teaspoons sugar
1 tablespoon dry sherry	1 tablespoon dry sherry
vegetable oil for deep-frying	vegetable oil for deep-frying
2 tomatoes	2 tomatoes
100 g/4 oz cabbage heart or spring greens	¼ lb cabbage heart or spring cabbage

Rub the chicken and cavity with salt and five-spice powder. Mix together the tangerine peel, onion, ginger, soy sauce, sugar and sherry. Coat the chicken with this mixture inside and out. Marinate for 8 hours. Remove the chicken, put it in a double boiler, cover and steam gently for 3½ hours.

Heat the oil in a deep-fat fryer to 180°C, 350°F, or until a day-old cube of bread turns golden in 1 minute. Gently lift out the hot chicken and drain in a wire basket for 1 minute. Hold the lid of the deep-fat fryer in one hand and with the other hand, plunge the wire basket with the chicken into the hot oil. Cover the deep-fat fryer for 2 minutes; remove the lid for 3 minutes. Remove the chicken, drain and place on a plate. Surround it with quartered tomatoes and shredded cabbage or spring greens.

Peking duck

(Illustrated on pages 26-27)

Peking K'ao Ya

This is a world famous dish. It owes its fascination and fame not only to the way it is cooked but also to the way it is eaten – wrapped in a doily (pancake) with a piece of spring onion or a strip of cucumber, and dabbed heavily with appropriate sauces. The combination of the duck, fresh, crunchy spring onion and strong, sweet, piquant sauces is delicious and unusual. The preparation and cooking of Peking duck may be very complicated or quite simple. The official version describing the preparation and cooking of this dish runs to over fifteen thousand words. This is the simplified version.

Serve for a banquet

METRIC/IMPERIAL	AMERICAN
1 (1·75-2·75-kg/4-6-lb) duckling	1 (4-6-lb) duckling
2 tablespoons castor sugar	3 tablespoons sugar
1 tablespoon dry sherry	1 tablespoon dry sherry
2 tablespoons water	3 tablespoons water
pinch salt	dash salt
30 doilies (see page 159)	30 doilies (see page 159)
15 spring onions or 1 cucumber	15 scallions or 1 cucumber
Garlic-vinegar dip	*Garlic-vinegar dip*
6 cloves garlic	6 cloves garlic
6 tablespoons vinegar	$\frac{1}{2}$ cup vinegar
Mustard-soy sauce dip	*Mustard-soy sauce dip*
1 teaspoon dry mustard	1 teaspoon dry mustard
2 tablespoons soy sauce	3 tablespoons soy sauce
Chilli-soy sauce dip	*Chili-soy sauce dip*
1 tablespoon chilli sauce	1 tablespoon chili sauce
3 tablespoons soy sauce	$\frac{1}{4}$ cup soy sauce

Clean the duck thoroughly and lower it momentarily into a pan of boiling water to scald. Dry immediately with absorbent kitchen paper and hang up by the feet to dry overnight in a cool, airy place. Alternatively, place in the refrigerator overnight.

Mix together the sugar, sherry, water and salt. Rub the outside of the duck with this sweetened water several hours before roasting. Hang up to dry again. When dry, give the duck a second rub over with sweetened water.

Preheat the oven to moderately hot (190°C, 375°F, Gas Mark 5). Place the duck in the oven on a rack with a roasting tin underneath to catch the drips. Roast for 20 minutes, then lower the temperature to cool (150°C, 300°F, Gas Mark 2) for 1 hour. Raise it again to moderately hot (200°C, 400°F, Gas Mark 6) for 20 minutes. The duck should then be well cooked and the skin very crisp. While the duck is cooking, prepare the doilies according to the instructions given, using double the quantities listed. Chop the spring onions into segments 5 cm/2 inches long. If using the cucumber, peel and cut into thin strips about 5 cm/2 inches long.

For the garlic-vinegar dip, crush the garlic cloves and mix with the vinegar. For the mustard-soy sauce dip, combine dry mustard with soy sauce.

For the chilli-soy sauce dip, combine the chilli sauce with the soy sauce.

Plum sauce (see page 162) and Haisein sauce (see page 160) are traditionally served with the dish.

Carving the duck is done at the dining table. At the first carving, only the skin is sliced off. Pieces of this are placed on a heated plate and passed around the table. Each diner opens a doily on his plate, dips one or two pieces of the skin in sauces of his choice (saucers of which are scattered over the table), and puts the skin on the doily. Finally, he places a piece of spring onion or a strip of cucumber on his doily, folds over the lower end and rolls up the doily. This is eaten with the fingers while the duck skin is still crackling and warm. Repeat the process until all the sliceable meat has been carved off the duck and each person has packed and eaten three to six doily rolls of duck skin and duck meat.

NOTE Although, traditionally, a person could eat a great deal more, this is not the only course in a Chinese meal or banquet. Quite often the guests are later treated to a soup made from the remains of the duck.

Stir-fried chicken with soy jam

Chiang Pao Chi Ting

This is a very popular and famous dish from the Ch'iu Hua Lo Restaurant, Peking.

Serve for a banquet or family meal

METRIC/IMPERIAL	AMERICAN
1 (175-g/6-oz) breast of chicken	1 (6-oz) chicken breast
1 egg white	1 egg white
1 tablespoon cornflour	1 tablespoon cornstarch
1 teaspoon ginger water (see page 160)	1 teaspoon ginger water (see page 160)
40 g/1½ oz lard	3 tablespoons lard
1½ tablespoons brown soy jam	2 tablespoons brown soy jam
1 teaspoon castor sugar	1 teaspoon sugar
1 tablespoon dry sherry	1 tablespoon dry sherry
½ teaspoon soft brown sugar	½ teaspoon soft brown sugar

Strip the chicken flesh from the bone and soak in cold water for 1 hour. Drain, dry and cut into 1-cm/½-inch cubes. Mix the egg white with 1 tablespoon of water in a bowl. Add the cornflour and blend to a thin batter. Add the chicken and mix evenly with your fingers. Prepare the ginger water according to instructions.

Heat two-thirds of the lard in a frying pan over low heat. When hot, add the chicken. Separate the cubes with a pair of chopsticks until they are well spread out. Stir-fry slowly for 1 minute. Remove the chicken with a perforated spoon and set aside.

Discard the lard from the pan and add the remaining lard. When melted, add the soy jam and stir until all moisture has evaporated (when the sizzling has almost stopped). Add the ginger water, sugar, sherry and brown sugar, and stir into a creamy paste. Add the partially-cooked chicken cubes. Stir and mix with the rich 'jam' over high heat for about 10-12 seconds, or until they are all glistening brown. If desired, add 1½ teaspoons lard. Let it melt completely and give everything a last stir. This adds to the general smoothness. Transfer to a heated, medium-sized flat plate and serve with rice.

Casserole of lion's heads

Sha Kuo Shih Tzu T'ou

Lion's heads are large meatballs cooked with 'stringy' vegetables, which together resemble the animal's head and mane.

Serve for a banquet or family meal

METRIC/IMPERIAL	AMERICAN
1 (675-g/1½-lb) belly of pork, coarsely minced	1 (1½-lb) salt pork, coarsely ground
1 egg	1 egg
2 tablespoons soy sauce	3 tablespoons soy sauce
1 teaspoon salt	1 teaspoon salt
2 tablespoons dry sherry	3 tablespoons dry sherry
1 tablespoon chopped onion	1 tablespoon chopped onion
1 teaspoon chopped fresh root ginger	1 teaspoon chopped fresh ginger root
2 tablespoons chopped bamboo shoots	3 tablespoons chopped bamboo shoots
1 tablespoon cornflour	1 tablespoon cornstarch
vegetable oil for deep-frying	vegetable oil for deep-frying
25 g/1 oz dried Chinese mushrooms, soaked and drained	1 cup dried Chinese mushrooms, soaked and drained
600 ml/1 pint secondary broth (see page 163)	2½ cups secondary broth (see page 163)
350 g/12 oz mustard cabbage or spinach	¾ lb mustard cabbage or spinach
25 g/1 oz lard	2 tablespoons lard

Mix together the minced pork, egg, half the soy sauce, half the salt, half the sherry, the onion, ginger, bamboo shoots and half the cornflour. Form the mixture into four large meatballs. Heat the oil to 180°C, 350°F, or until a day-old cube of bread turns golden in 1 minute. Place the meatballs in a wire basket and deep-fry until golden. Drain. Thinly slice the mushrooms.

Heat the broth in a flameproof casserole. Add the remaining salt, sherry, soy sauce and the mushrooms. Place the meatballs in the broth. Bring to the boil and simmer gently for 45 minutes. Discard the thicker stalks from the mustard cabbage. Sauté the cabbage in the lard for 2 minutes. Add to the meatballs. Cover and simmer for a further 10 minutes.

Remove the lid of the casserole. Lift out the mustard cabbage and arrange around the sides of a large heated serving dish. Place the meatballs in the centre. Mix the remaining cornflour in 1 tablespoon of water and add to the broth in the casserole. Heat, stirring until thickened, and pour over the meatballs.

Yellow 'flower' meat

Mu Hsu Jou

A popular dish with the people of Peking and the north, this is a scrambled omelette cooked with a limited amount of shredded meat and one or two other ingredients. This is really a rice-eater's dish and very much one for home cooking.

Serve for a family meal

METRIC/IMPERIAL	AMERICAN
4 eggs	4 eggs
$\frac{1}{2}$ teaspoon salt	$\frac{1}{2}$ teaspoon salt
100 g/4 oz lean pork	$\frac{1}{4}$ lb lean pork
8 dried Chinese mushrooms, soaked and drained	8 dried Chinese mushrooms, soaked and drained
3 spring onions	3 scallions
4 tablespoons vegetable oil	$\frac{1}{3}$ cup vegetable oil
1 tablespoon soy sauce	1 tablespoon soy sauce
2 tablespoons broth (superior or secondary, see pages 170 and 163)	3 tablespoons broth (superior or secondary, see pages 170 and 163)
$\frac{1}{2}$ teaspoon monosodium glutamate (optional)	$\frac{1}{2}$ teaspoon monosodium glutamate (optional)
1 teaspoon castor sugar	1 teaspoon sugar
1 tablespoon dry sherry	1 tablespoon dry sherry
1 teaspoon sesame oil	1 teaspoon sesame oil

Beat the eggs in a bowl for a few seconds and add the salt. Shred the pork into matchstick-thin strips. Cut the mushrooms into thin strips or small pieces. Cut the spring onions into very thin slices. Heat half the oil in a frying pan and add the beaten egg. Lower the heat (so that none of the egg will burn) and just before the egg sets completely, scramble slightly. Remove from the pan and set aside.

Add the remaining oil to the frying pan and turn the heat to high. Add the pork, mushrooms and spring onions. Sauté for 2 minutes, then add the soy sauce, broth, monosodium glutamate and sugar. Cook for a further 30-40 seconds. Add the scrambled egg, sherry and sesame oil. Stir gently to mix all the ingredients. Serve on a heated dish.

Peking dust

Li Tzu Fen

Towards the end of spring, after a rainless autumn and winter, the North China Plain is very dry and dust storms often blow in from the Inner Mongolian desert. But the 'Peking dust' here is made from chestnuts.

Serve to conclude a banquet or family party

METRIC/IMPERIAL	AMERICAN
900 g/2 lb chestnuts	2 lb chestnuts
$\frac{1}{2}$ teaspoon salt	$\frac{1}{2}$ teaspoon salt
150 g/5 oz castor sugar	$\frac{2}{3}$ cup sugar
300 ml/$\frac{1}{2}$ pint double cream	$1\frac{1}{4}$ cups heavy cream
vanilla essence (optional)	vanilla extract (optional)
6-8 pieces crystallised fruit	6-8 pieces crystallised fruit

Make a criss-cross cut on the flat side of each of the chestnuts. Plunge them into boiling water and cook for 40 minutes. Drain, remove the shells and skins and mash the chestnuts finely. Blend in the salt and half the sugar. Whip the cream in a separate bowl and fold in the remaining sugar (and a little vanilla essence to taste, if desired).

Form a mound of chestnut 'dust' in a bowl for each diner. Top with the whipped cream and garnish with crystallised fruit.

Drawn-thread honeyed apples

Pa Ssu P'ing Kuo

The Chinese do not have many desserts in their culinary repertoire, but this unusual one has gained in popularity. The contrast in textures of the crispy toffee and soft apple is one of the charms of the dish.

Serve for a banquet or family meal

METRIC/IMPERIAL	AMERICAN
900 g/2 lb apples	2 lb apples
1 egg	1 egg
2 tablespoons plain flour	3 tablespoons all-purpose flour
vegetable oil for deep-frying	vegetable oil for deep-frying
4 tablespoons castor sugar	$\frac{1}{3}$ cup sugar
2 tablespoons vegetable oil	3 tablespoons vegetable oil
3 tablespoons water	$\frac{1}{4}$ cup water
3 tablespoons golden syrup	$\frac{1}{4}$ cup corn syrup

Peel and core the apples. Cut into 3×1-cm/$1\frac{1}{2} \times \frac{1}{2}$-inch 'chips'. Beat the egg. Dip the 'chips' in the egg and dredge with flour. Heat the oil to 180°C, 350°F, or until a day-old cube of bread turns golden in 1 minute. Deep-fry the 'chips' for $2\frac{1}{2}$ minutes, then drain. Heat the sugar and the 2 tablespoons vegetable oil in a flameproof dish. When the sugar has melted, add the water, followed by the syrup. Continue to stir gently over the heat until the liquid has become golden. Add the apple 'chips' to the hot syrup, turning the pieces over so that they are well coated. Bring to the table in the cooking dish.

Each diner should be provided with a bowl of water with ice floating in it. Using his chopsticks, he draws a piece of apple from the dish and plunges it into the water. The coating syrup instantly cools into a brittle hardness. After the dipping, the apple should be placed in a saucer to cool for a few moments before eating. In the process of dipping, the apple should not be left for any length of time in the water as it will become sodden.

Ice-mountain fruit salad

(Illustrated on page 28)

Ts'uan Ping Wan

This cold sweet dish appears in Peking towards early summer, usually to begin a meal – almost as an aperitif. Sliced fresh lotus roots, fresh water chestnuts and peaches are often used. Here in the West, there is no reason why strawberries and pineapples should not be used.

Serve for a banquet or family meal

METRIC/IMPERIAL	AMERICAN
450 g/1 lb apples	1 lb apples
450 g/1 lb pears	1 lb pears
450 g/1 lb peaches	1 lb peaches
1 honeydew melon	1 honeydew melon
450 g/1 lb cherries	1 lb cherries
450 g/1 lb strawberries	1 lb strawberries
450 g/1 lb grapes	1 lb grapes
225 g/8 oz water chestnuts	$\frac{1}{2}$ lb water chestnuts
1 small pineapple	1 small pineapple
crushed ice (see recipe)	crushed ice (see recipe)

Peel the apples, pears and peaches. Cut them into quarters. Place in iced water (to prevent browning) while preparing the other fruits. Halve the melon, remove the seeds and cut the flesh into similar-sized pieces. Rinse and stone the cherries and hull the strawberries. Peel and de-seed the grapes. Slice the water chestnuts. Peel and slice the pineapple, removing the woody centre part.

Make a bed of crushed ice on a very large serving plate. Arrange the pieces of fruit on top in an artistic pattern, interspersing the fruits with larger chunks of ice. Alternatively, a raised mound of ice may be piled in the middle of the large serving plate to give the effect of a miniature ice-mountain. Decorate the ice-mountain with the fruit.

NOTE Small saucers with sugar or with a mixture of sugar and ground ginger may be used as dips.

Shantung and Hopei

As I remember it, Shantung is very much a 'chicken country'. Every time the train stopped at Tsinan or Techow on our journey to college in the early autumn, we would each pick up a roast chicken from the vendors along the railway line and munch it on the way. Of course, it can be said that every part of China is 'chicken country', but Shantung seems to be more so than any other. It is also a great cotton and peanut producing area, apart from cultivating large crops of fruit such as pears, peaches, apples, grapes and melons.

The centre of the province is a mountainous ridge which becomes a peninsula in the North China Sea. The Yellow River used to flow south of the province into the sea, but a century ago it changed its course to the north by several hundred miles. In spite of the favourable climate, the region has had its share of natural disasters.

The lower reaches of the Yellow River were, in fact, the cradle of China's history and civilization. Both Confucius and Mencius were born and lived here, as did Laotse, the founder of the Taoist School of Philosophy. It is little wonder that all the cooking of North China, including Peking cuisine, derived much of its inspiration from these two provinces.

The Chinese from this region are particularly tall and heavy in build (six-footers are common). This often surprises westerners, used to the Chinese from Hong Kong and Canton who are usually only slightly bigger than the Vietnamese.

The province immediately north of Shantung is Hopei, in which the capital city of Peking is situated. Here the seaboard is flatter and muddy. It is along this coast that the large North China prawns abound. They, together with the freshwater crabs, are a characteristic part of the diet and delicacies of the region. Hopei is bordered in the west and north by the famous Great Wall, which divides it from Manchuria to the north and much of Inner Mongolia to the northwest. Immediately north of the Wall, one can perceive the aridness of the Gobi desert. South of the Wall the land is quite lush and here in this wheat and corn producing region the basic diet is more often steamed bread *(mun-tao)* than rice. It is usually accompanied by strong-tasting vegetables such as leeks, garlic, shallots and onions, as well as a little meat, and frequent and generous amounts of soy jam. Meat and chicken are often cooked and eaten plain (boiled, roasted or barbecued), but they are made more tasty by dipping them in various types of 'mixes' and sauces on the table, such as salt-pepper mix, chilli-soy sauce mix, garlic-vinegar mix, ginger-vinegar mix, Plum sauce, sweetened soy jam or Haisein sauce. Many people who are brought up on, or have grown used to, this strong, chunky, hearty food much prefer it to what they consider the fussier products of the southern kitchens.

North Chinese fried potato chips

Ch'ao Tu Tou Ssu

When eaten at a meal in China, chips — like all other dishes — are meant to accompany rice and are treated like any other savoury vegetable dish.

Serve for a family meal

METRIC/IMPERIAL	AMERICAN
450 g/1 lb large potatoes	1 lb large potatoes
1 chilli pepper	1 chili pepper
3 tablespoons vegetable oil	$\frac{1}{4}$ cup vegetable oil
1 tablespoon chopped onion	1 tablespoon chopped onion
1 tablespoon soy sauce	1 tablespoon soy sauce
$\frac{1}{2}$ teaspoon salt	$\frac{1}{2}$ teaspoon salt
$1\frac{1}{2}$ teaspoons vinegar	$1\frac{1}{2}$ teaspoons vinegar

Peel the potatoes and cut lengthwise into thin slices. Place the slices on top of each other and cut into long, matchstick-thin chips. Simmer the chips in boiling water for 2 minutes and drain. De-seed and chop the chilli pepper.

Heat the oil in a frying pan over high heat. Sauté the chilli pepper in it for 15 seconds, then add the onion and sauté for another 30 seconds. Discard the pepper and onion. Add the potato chips. Toss and turn the chips in the oil for 3 minutes. Add the soy sauce, salt and vinegar. Continue to stir-fry, but more gently, for 1 minute and then drain on absorbent kitchen paper. Transfer to a flat, well-heated serving dish.

Coral-coloured cabbage

Shan Hu Pai T'sai

The Tai An *variety of Chinese celery cabbage is particularly well-known in North China. The dish is so called because of its crimson coral colour. This recipe comes from the county* Tai An, *Shantung.*

Serve for a banquet or family party

METRIC/IMPERIAL	AMERICAN
1 (900-g/2-lb) Chinese celery cabbage (see page 157)	1 (2-lb) Chinese celery cabbage (see page 157)
75 g/3 oz bamboo shoots	$\frac{3}{4}$ cup bamboo shoots
4-6 dried Chinese mushrooms, soaked and drained	4-6 dried Chinese mushrooms, soaked and drained
1 large sweet red pepper	1 large sweet red pepper
$\frac{1}{2}$ chilli pepper	$\frac{1}{2}$ chili pepper
1 teaspoon salt	1 teaspoon salt
2 tablespoons sesame oil	3 tablespoons sesame oil
1 tablespoon soy sauce	1 tablespoon soy sauce
2 tablespoons castor sugar	3 tablespoons sugar
$1\frac{1}{2}$ tablespoons vinegar	2 tablespoons vinegar
1 tablespoon tomato purée	1 tablespoon tomato paste
4 tablespoons water	$\frac{1}{3}$ cup water

Remove and discard the outer leaves of the cabbage and reserve only the heart. Cut each heart vertically into four and then again into pieces 3-5 cm/ $1\frac{1}{2}$-2 inches long. Slice the bamboo shoots and mushrooms into matchstick-thin strips. Remove the seeds from the sweet pepper and chilli pepper and slice in the same manner.

Plunge the cabbage into boiling water for 3 minutes. Drain and sprinkle with salt. Arrange in an orderly pattern on a large heated serving plate and keep warm.

Heat the sesame oil in a large frying pan. Add the prepared peppers, bamboo shoots and mushrooms. Then stir-fry over high heat for 2 minutes. Add the soy sauce, sugar, vinegar and tomato purée. Continue to stir-fry for 1 minute. Add the water and simmer for 3 minutes. Mix well and pour over the cabbage as a hot garnish.

Stew-braised beef with tomato

Hsi Hung Shih Men Niu Jou

This is an economical dish as the meat is an inexpensive cut. Together with broth and tomato, it makes an extremely tasty dish to accompany rice. The broth resulting from boiling the beef may be used separately with additional seasoning to make an excellent soup.

Serve for a family meal

METRIC/IMPERIAL	AMERICAN
675 g/1½ lb shin of beef	1½ lb boneless chuck
900 ml/1½ pints water	3¾ cups water
225 g/8 oz tomatoes	½ lb tomatoes
2 tablespoons castor sugar	3 tablespoons sugar
2 cloves garlic	2 cloves garlic
vegetable oil for deep-frying	vegetable oil for deep-frying
3 slices fresh root ginger	3 slices fresh ginger root
1 tablespoon chopped onion	1 tablespoon chopped onion
1 tablespoon vegetable oil	1 tablespoon vegetable oil
2 tablespoons soy sauce	3 tablespoons soy sauce
1½ tablespoons dry sherry	2 tablespoons dry sherry
150 ml/¼ pint superior broth (see page 170)	⅔ cup superior broth (see page 170)
1 tablespoon cornflour	1 tablespoon cornstarch
½ teaspoon monosodium glutamate (optional)	½ teaspoon monosodium glutamate (optional)
2 tablespoons water	3 tablespoons water
½ teaspoon chilli sauce	½ teaspoon chili sauce

Place the beef in a saucepan with the water, bring to the boil, cover and simmer gently for 2½ hours. When the beef is tender, drain and cut into 2·5-cm/1-inch cubes. Scald the tomatoes in boiling water. Drain, peel, cut into quarters and remove the seeds. Place the tomatoes in a saucepan, add half the sugar and simmer for 10 minutes until reduced to a purée. Pour this sweetened purée into a bowl. Crush the garlic.

Heat the oil to 180°C, 350°F, or until a day-old cube of bread turns golden in 1 minute. Deep-fry the beef cubes for 1½ minutes. Drain the meat and set aside. Sauté the garlic, ginger and onion in the 1 tablespoon of oil for 1 minute over medium heat. Add the remaining sugar, soy sauce, sherry and superior broth. Add the beef and simmer for 5 minutes. Then add the tomato purée and simmer for 3 minutes. Blend the cornflour and monosodium glutamate with the water. Add to the beef and stir over the heat. Sprinkle with the chilli sauce and serve.

Right *Double-cooked steamed pork with pickled salted cabbage (see page 64).*
Overleaf *Hot-braised sliced beef (see page 56); Quick-fried ribbon of duck (see page 61); T'ung Ching vegetarian noodles (see page 69).*

Sweet and sour Yellow River carp

Huang Ho T'ang T'su Li Yu

*The Yellow River carp is a delicacy often mentioned in Chinese literature.
The leftovers, including head and tail, are traditionally made into a sweet
and sour soup.*

Serve for a banquet

METRIC/IMPERIAL	AMERICAN
1 (450-900-g/1-2-lb) carp	1 (1-2-lb) carp
1½ teaspoons salt	1½ teaspoons salt
50 g/2 oz plain flour	½ cup all-purpose flour
vegetable oil for deep-frying	vegetable oil for deep-frying
Sauce	*Sauce*
1 tablespoon chopped spring onion	1 tablespoon chopped scallion
2 teaspoons chopped fresh root ginger	2 teaspoons chopped fresh ginger root
1 clove garlic	1 clove garlic
5 water chestnuts	5 water chestnuts
40 g/1½ oz bamboo shoots	2 bamboo shoots
15 g/½ oz wood-ears, soaked and drained	½ cup wood-ears, soaked and drained
6 tablespoons superior broth (see page 170)	½ cup superior broth (see page 170)
1 tablespoon soy sauce	1 tablespoon soy sauce
1½ tablespoons wine vinegar	2 tablespoons wine vinegar
2 tablespoons castor sugar	3 tablespoons sugar
2 tablespoons dry sherry	3 tablespoons dry sherry
2 teaspoons cornflour	2 teaspoons cornstarch
2 tablespoons vegetable oil	3 tablespoons vegetable oil

Gut, scale and wash the fish thoroughly. Slash it on both sides at 2·5-cm/
1-inch intervals and about 5 mm/¼ inch deep. Rub inside and outside with
salt and let stand for 20 minutes. Then coat the fish in the flour. To make
the sauce, place the spring onion and ginger in a bowl. Crush the garlic
and add to the bowl. Thinly slice the water chestnuts and bamboo shoots
and put them in a second bowl together with the wood-ears. Mix the cold
broth, soy sauce, vinegar, sugar, sherry and cornflour in a third bowl.

Heat the oil to 180°C, 350°F, or until a day-old cube of bread turns golden
in 1 minute. Place the fish in a wire basket and deep-fry for about 10 minutes
or until crisp and golden. Meanwhile, sauté the spring onion, ginger and
garlic in the 2 tablespoons oil over high heat for 1 minute. Add the bamboo
shoots, water chestnuts and wood-ears, then stir-fry for 30 seconds. Pour
in the broth mixture from the third bowl. Stir and leave for 1 minute.
Drain the fish, arrange on a heated serving dish and immediately pour over
the sauce.

The cooking of the fish and the sauce should be timed so that the fish will
crackle audibly when the sauce is poured over. The fish is best served
immediately.

Left *Red-cooked pork with chestnuts (see page 55).*

49

Quick-stirred dry-fried shrimps

Kan Shao Hsia Jen

The aim of this recipe is to cook a dish of shrimps with as few other ingredients as possible. In the finishing stages, there is no sauce in the pan and very little oil. The shrimps are largely on their own, their taste heightened only by the heat and the flavour of spring onion and ginger. Chef Yuan, whose recipe this is, does not believe in the use of monosodium glutamate.

Serve for a banquet or family meal

METRIC/IMPERIAL	AMERICAN
900 g/2 lb cooked shrimps	2 lb cooked shrimps
1 teaspoon salt	1 teaspoon salt
1 tablespoon dry sherry	1 tablespoon dry sherry
1 egg	1 egg
1½ teaspoons cornflour	1½ teaspoons cornstarch
100 g/4 oz lard	½ cup lard
1 tablespoon chopped spring onion	1 tablespoon chopped scallion
1 teaspoon chopped fresh root ginger	1 teaspoon chopped fresh ginger root
1½ teaspoons light-coloured soy sauce	1½ teaspoons light-colored soy sauce

Mix the shrimps carefully in a bowl with the salt, half the sherry, the egg and cornflour. Heat the lard in a large frying pan until very hot. Add the shrimps and stir-fry quickly over high heat. After 45 seconds, remove the shrimps and set aside.

Add the spring onion, ginger, remaining sherry and soy sauce. Stir-fry quickly again over high heat for 20 seconds. Return the shrimps to the pan and stir-fry more gently for another 20 seconds.

The shrimps should be served in a heated dish and eaten immediately.

Apple-chicken

Ping-Kuo Chi

This recipe is from the Yen Hsi Tang dining rooms in Tsinan. It is a slightly unusual dish mainly because of its extraordinary combination—chicken and apple—as well as its unique presentation; using chicken meat and other ingredients to stuff the apple.

Serve for a banquet or family meal

METRIC/IMPERIAL	AMERICAN
350 g/12 oz chicken	$1\frac{1}{2}$ cups chicken
40 g/1$\frac{1}{2}$ oz ham	$\frac{1}{4}$ cup ham
40 g/1$\frac{1}{2}$ oz dried Chinese mushrooms, soaked and drained	$1\frac{1}{2}$ cups dried Chinese mushrooms, soaked and drained
40 g/1$\frac{1}{2}$ oz water chestnuts	$\frac{1}{4}$ cup water chestnuts
1$\frac{1}{2}$ teaspoons castor sugar	1$\frac{1}{2}$ teaspoons sugar
1 tablespoon soy sauce	1 tablespoon soy sauce
1 tablespoon onion oil (see note)	1 tablespoon onion oil (see note)
1 tablespoon chilli-sherry (see note)	1 tablespoon chili-sherry (see note)
1 teaspoon monosodium glutamate (optional)	1 teaspoon monosodium glutamate (optional)
6 even-sized cooking apples	6 even-sized baking apples
300 ml/$\frac{1}{2}$ pint superior broth (see page 170)	1$\frac{1}{4}$ cups superior broth (see page 170)
2 teaspoons cornflour	2 teaspoons cornstarch

Cut the chicken flesh into 3·5-cm × 5-cm × 5-mm/1$\frac{1}{2}$ × 2 × $\frac{1}{4}$-inch wide strips. Slice the ham, mushrooms and water chestnuts into matchstick-thin strips. Place all the chopped ingredients into a bowl and add half the sugar, half the soy sauce, half the onion oil, half the chilli-sherry and half the monosodium glutamate and leave to marinate for 30 minutes.

Slice the tops off the apples and reserve as lids. Core the apples leaving the base intact and widen the hole to about 2·5 cm/1 inch square. Peel the apples and dip each one into boiling water for 10 seconds. Allow to drain.

Stuff the apples with the marinating ingredients, pouring in any left-over marinating juice. Place the reserved lids on the apples and secure with a cocktail stick. Place the apples on to an ovenproof dish, put into a steamer and steam for 1$\frac{1}{4}$ hours.

Meanwhile, make the sauce. Bring the superior broth to the boil, remove from the heat then add the remaining sugar, soy sauce, onion oil and chilli-sherry. Mix the cornflour with a little water and add to the sauce with the remaining monosodium glutamate. Bring the mixture back to the boil stirring constantly and pour over the apples to serve immediately.

NOTE   To make the onion oil, fry 1 tablespoon chopped onion in 2 tablespoons (U.S. 3 tablespoons) oil for 1 minute and strain for liquid. To make the chilli-sherry, soak 1 teaspoon dried chilli pepper in 4 tablespoons (U.S. $\frac{1}{3}$ cup) sherry overnight and strain for liquid.

Szechwan

In population, Szechwan is the largest single province of China. Historically, the area was practically unknown until the latter part of the Han Dynasty (206 B.C.–A.D. 221). By the time of the 'Three Kingdoms' (A.D. 221-317), it was already referred to in the literature of the day as 'Heaven's own mansion' (or in western terms, 'God's own country') 'where stretches of fertile fields roll away by the thousand miles'. Szechwan is very well endowed, for, apart from producing quantities of rice, wheat, corn and cotton, it also produces silk, salt and practically the whole gamut of the fruits which are popular in China. But, above all, to the world at large, Szechwan is best known for the panda, which lives in the bamboo forests in the western parts of the province.

With large grain crops, there are naturally plenty of pigs and poultry. Since almost all fertile and arable lands are cultivated, there is not much grazing land. Consequently, this is not sheep country and lamb is not used as extensively as in the North. On the other hand, it is a little surprising to find that there are quite a number of beef dishes among the native Szechwan recipes. This is supposedly because in the extensive salt mines of Szechwan, the haulage is done by oxen or steers, because of the breeding of cattle for this purpose. Many of them, in the end, land in dishes on the dining table. In spite of it being so far inland and land-locked, there are numerous rivers, ponds and tributaries where there is no lack of freshwater fish, duck or even shrimps.

In the summer, Szechwan is a very hot country. It is not surprising that the people of Szechwan like their food hot and peppery, as in many tropical countries. A particularly hot and strongly-flavoured pepper is used in some dishes but anyone not familiar with this fiery spice is advised to treat it with respect – at first the hotness is not apparent, but suddenly it burns the mouth with unbelievable ferocity. Salt is used extensively in their dishes and perhaps with more skill and effect than elsewhere. As a by-product of salt, Szechwan also produces an exceptional range of pickles, which are often used in cooking fresh food to give added piquancy. Perhaps, because of the abundance of chicken and duck, their fats are used more often in Szechwan than elsewhere to cook various vegetable and meat dishes. Being fertile and semi-tropical, there is naturally a very wide range of vegetables, plants and fungi and a sizeable range of medicinal herbs.

One method of cooking frequently used here is smoking. Quick-frying over a high fire, which is a popular form of cooking in almost every other part of China, is not the predominant style of cooking in Szechwan kitchens. Steaming, simmering and hot-assembly are mainly used. The diet and dishes of Szechwan seem to reflect, more than any other provincial cooking, the range and balance of Chinese cooking as a whole.

Chengtu

Yangtze

Chungking

Fried winter bamboo shoots with pickled salted cabbage

Yen Pai T'sai Tung Sun

This recipe uses the popular Szechwan salted cabbage to give a highly savoury flavour to the bamboo and chicken. It is ideal to accompany rice and meat dishes.

Serve for a family meal

METRIC/IMPERIAL	AMERICAN
675 g/1½ lb winter bamboo shoots	6 cups winter bamboo shoots
40 g/1½ oz pickled Szechwan cabbage (see page 162)	⅓ cup pickled Szechwan cabbage (see page 162)
25 g/1 oz lard	2 tablespoons lard
6 tablespoons chicken broth	½ cup chicken broth
1 teaspoon salt	1 teaspoon salt
2 tablespoons dry sherry	3 tablespoons dry sherry
1 teaspoon monosodium glutamate (optional)	1 teaspoon monosodium glutamate (optional)
½ tablespoon cornflour	1½ teaspoons cornstarch
1½ tablespoons water	2 tablespoons water
15 g/½ oz chicken fat	1 tablespoon chicken fat

Remove and discard the outer layers of the bamboo shoots and reserve the softer hearts. Slice these lengthwise into 0.5×1-cm/$\frac{1}{4} \times \frac{1}{2}$-inch wide strips and then cut into 3×5-cm/$1\frac{1}{2} \times 2$-inch segments. Finely chop the pickled salted cabbage.

Heat the lard in a frying pan. When hot, pour in the bamboo shoots and stir-fry for 1 minute. Remove the bamboo shoots and set aside. Sauté the pickled salted cabbage in the lard remaining in the pan for 1 minute over medium heat. Return the bamboo shoots to the pan and stir-fry together with the cabbage for 1 minute.

Pour in the chicken broth, salt, sherry and monosodium glutamate. Simmer for 3 minutes. Add the cornflour blended with the water. Continue to stir-fry gently. Add the chicken fat in small pieces before serving on a heated flat dish.

Red-cooked pork with chestnuts

(Illustrated on page 48)

Pan Li Shao Jou

Chestnuts, like peanuts, are often used with meat in China. The process of red-cooking is like ordinary stewing, except for the use of soy sauce.

Serve for a family meal or party

METRIC/IMPERIAL	AMERICAN
900 g/2 lb belly of pork	2 lb salt pork
1 small onion	1 small onion
450 g/1 lb chestnuts	1 lb chestnuts
2 tablespoons vegetable oil	3 tablespoons vegetable oil
3 slices fresh root ginger	3 slices fresh ginger root
$\frac{1}{2}$ teaspoon salt	$\frac{1}{2}$ teaspoon salt
2 tablespoons soy sauce	3 tablespoons soy sauce
450 ml/$\frac{3}{4}$ pint secondary broth	2 cups secondary broth (see page 163)
(see page 163)	1 tablespoon sugar
1 tablespoon castor sugar	3 tablespoons dry sherry
2 tablespoons dry sherry	

Wash the pork in hot water and cut into 2·5-cm/1-inch cubes so that each piece has lean meat and fat. Peel and quarter the onion. Slash the chestnuts and then cook in boiling water for 20-25 minutes. Drain and remove the skins. Heat the oil in a heavy saucepan. Sauté the onion and ginger for 1 minute over medium heat. Add the pork and, raising the heat to high, stir-fry for 3 minutes. Add the salt and half the soy sauce. Stir-fry for 3 more minutes. Pour in the broth. Bring to the boil, lower the heat as far as it will go, and simmer, covered, for 45 minutes, turning the meat over three or four times in the process.

Add the chestnuts, remaining soy sauce, sugar and sherry. Continue with the slow-simmering for another 30 minutes, mixing the chestnuts with the meat and turning the mixture over gently three or four times in the process. Serve with rice.

Hot-braised sliced beef

(Illustrated on pages 46–47)

Sui Chu Niu Jou

It is the usual process in Chinese cooking for quick-frying to be followed by a period of braise-simmering, when a little broth is added to the food. This recipe is a typical example of this method.

Serve for a banquet or family meal

METRIC/IMPERIAL	AMERICAN
450 g/1 lb rump steak	1 lb beef tenderloin
1 egg	1 egg
25 g/1 oz cornflour	$\frac{1}{4}$ cup cornstarch
1 teaspoon salt	1 teaspoon salt
4 teaspoons dried chilli peppers	4 teaspoons dried chili peppers
1 small sweet green or red pepper	1 small sweet green or red pepper
5 tablespoons vegetable oil	6 tablespoons vegetable oil
1 tablespoon fermented black beans, soaked for 1 hour (see page 156)	1 tablespoon fermented black beans, soaked for 1 hour (see page 156)
50 g/2 oz bamboo shoots	$\frac{1}{2}$ cup bamboo shoots
3 spring onions	3 scallions
1 tablespoon chopped onion	1 tablespoon chopped onion
1 tablespoon chopped fresh root ginger	1 tablespoon chopped fresh ginger root
1 small leek, trimmed and sliced	1 small leek, trimmed and sliced
$\frac{1}{4}$ teaspoon freshly ground black pepper	$\frac{1}{4}$ teaspoon freshly ground black pepper
1 tablespoon dry sherry	1 tablespoon dry sherry
2 tablespoons white wine	3 tablespoons white wine
150 ml/$\frac{1}{4}$ pint superior broth (see page 170)	$\frac{2}{3}$ cup superior broth (see page 170)
1 teaspoon monosodium glutamate (optional)	1 teaspoon monosodium glutamate (optional)

Cut the steak into thin 2·5 × 3-cm/1 × 1$\frac{1}{2}$-inch slices. Break the egg into a bowl. Add the cornflour and salt. Blend to a smooth batter. Mix in the beef, using your fingers to coat the meat evenly with the batter.

Remove and discard the seeds from the chilli and sweet peppers. Slice the sweet pepper into strips. Stir-fry in half the oil for 1$\frac{1}{2}$ minutes and set aside. Mash the fermented beans. Cut the bamboo shoots and spring onions into 3-cm/1$\frac{1}{2}$-inch segments.

Heat the remaining oil in a large frying pan. Add the black beans, bamboo shoots, spring onions, onion, ginger, leek and pepper, and stir-fry slowly over medium heat for 2 minutes. Add the sherry and wine and, after 10 seconds, add the broth and monosodium glutamate. Turn the heat to high. When the contents reboil, add the coated beef. After 30 seconds of stir-braising, transfer to a deep serving dish. Meanwhile, reheat the chilli and sweet peppers and arrange them, together with the oil, on the beef.

Double-cooked pork

Hui Kuo Jou

Double-cooked pork is said to have been first invented in Szechwan, although it is now popular throughout China. It is not exactly a delicacy, but because of the attractive green and red-brown colour combination, it is sometimes included at a dinner party. This recipe comes from the Fei Yung Dining Rooms, Chengtu.

Serve for a family meal or party

METRIC/IMPERIAL	AMERICAN
900 g/2 lb chump end or loin of pork	2 lb butt end or pork loin
1 small leek	1 small leek
1 tablespoon fermented black beans, soaked for 1 hour (see page 156)	1 tablespoon fermented black beans, soaked for 1 hour (see page 156)
15 g/$\frac{1}{2}$ oz lard	1 tablespoon lard
1$\frac{1}{2}$ teaspoons castor sugar	1$\frac{1}{2}$ teaspoons sugar
1 tablespoon soy sauce	1 tablespoon soy sauce
1 teaspoon chilli sauce	1 teaspoon chili sauce
2 teaspoons Plum or Haisein sauce (see pages 162 or 160)	2 teaspoons Plum or Haisein sauce (see pages 162 or 160)

Boil the pork in water to cover for 20 minutes. Drain and cool for 30 minutes. Remove the rind and cut the pork into 2·5 × 3-cm/1 × 1$\frac{1}{2}$-inch slices. Each slice should have both lean meat and fat. Trim the leek so that there are equal parts of green and white. Cut into 3-cm/1$\frac{1}{2}$-inch long segments. Mash the fermented beans into a paste.

Heat the lard in a frying pan. Add the pork and cook for 2 minutes over low heat. Add the sugar, soy sauce, chilli sauce and Plum or Haisein sauce, and turn the heat to high. After 20 seconds of quick-stir-frying, add the leeks and continue to stir-fry for 1$\frac{1}{2}$ minutes. Transfer to a heated dish to serve.

NOTE The resulting dish is both sweet and salty and it is extremely savoury. It is another of those Chinese dishes where the final hot-frying over high heat with a leek (or onion) gives it a special appeal, and the heat itself is considered part of the attraction.

Kung-po hot-fried kidney

Kung-Po Yao Kuai

Kung-po hot-frying is a method brought to Szechwan from Peking, but in Szechwan it is even hotter! This dish tastes salty, sweet, sour and hot all at the same time.

Serve for a banquet

METRIC/IMPERIAL	AMERICAN
350 g/12 oz pig's kidneys	$\frac{3}{4}$ lb pork kidney
1$\frac{1}{2}$ tablespoons cornflour	2 tablespoons cornstarch
1$\frac{1}{2}$ tablespoons dry sherry	2 tablespoons dry sherry
$\frac{1}{2}$ teaspoon salt	$\frac{1}{2}$ teaspoon salt
1 tablespoon castor sugar	1 tablespoon sugar
1 tablespoon vinegar	1 tablespoon vinegar
1 tablespoon soy sauce	1 tablespoon soy sauce
$\frac{1}{2}$ teaspoon monosodium glutamate (optional)	$\frac{1}{2}$ teaspoon monosodium glutamate (optional)
2 tablespoons superior broth (see page 170)	3 tablespoons superior broth (see page 170)
3 spring onions	3 scallions
1 dried chilli pepper	1 dried chili pepper
1 small leek	1 small leek
4-5 tablespoons vegetable oil	$\frac{1}{3}$ cup vegetable oil
2 cloves garlic	2 cloves garlic
3 slices fresh root ginger	3 slices fresh ginger root
$\frac{1}{4}$ teaspoon chilli powder	$\frac{1}{4}$ teaspoon chili powder
freshly ground black pepper	freshly ground black pepper

Remove and discard the core and cut each kidney in half. Slash with criss-cross cuts 5 mm/$\frac{1}{2}$ cm apart and two-thirds through the kidney. Cut into 1·5 × 2·5-cm/$\frac{3}{4}$ × 1-inch pieces. Blend half the cornflour with 1 tablespoon of water, the sherry and salt. Thoroughly coat the kidney pieces in this mixture. In a separate bowl, mix the sugar, vinegar, soy sauce, monosodium glutamate and broth. Set aside. Cut the spring onions into 1-cm/$\frac{1}{2}$-inch pieces. Remove and discard the seeds from the chilli pepper. Cut the leek into 1-cm/$\frac{1}{2}$-inch pieces.

  Heat the oil in a frying pan until very hot. Add the kidney, spreading the pieces evenly, sauté for 15 seconds and then put aside. Discard the excess oil. In the same pan, sauté the chilli pepper for 1 minute and discard. Crush the garlic, then stir-fry the spring onions, leek, garlic, ginger and chilli powder for 20 seconds. Add the kidney pieces and stir-fry for 10 seconds. Gradually add the vinegar mixture. Pour this slowly from the bowl into the pan. Stir-fry the kidney gently for 15 seconds. Add pepper to taste and serve immediately.

Hot diced chicken in ground peanuts

Sui Mi Chi Ting

A fairly universal method of preparing chicken in China is by cooking it diced in cubes. This is really the Peking method. Many Peking high officials and emissaries were appointed to Szechwan, and exercised a considerable influence there in culinary, as well as other matters. This recipe is for a Peking-style dish, cooked with local Szechwan materials like peanuts and hot seasonings.

Serve for a banquet or family meal

METRIC/IMPERIAL	AMERICAN
3 large breasts of chicken	3 large chicken breasts
1 tablespoon cornflour	1 tablespoon cornstarch
1 egg	1 egg
40 g/$1\frac{1}{2}$ oz peanuts	$\frac{1}{2}$ cup peanuts
2 spring onions	2 scallions
1 tablespoon water	1 tablespoon water
$1\frac{1}{2}$ teaspoons castor sugar	$1\frac{1}{2}$ teaspoons sugar
2 teaspoons vinegar	2 teaspoons vinegar
$1\frac{1}{2}$ teaspoons soy sauce	$1\frac{1}{2}$ teaspoons soy sauce
$\frac{1}{2}$ teaspoon salt	$\frac{1}{2}$ teaspoon salt
vegetable oil for deep-frying	vegetable oil for deep-frying
4 teaspoons dried chilli peppers	4 teaspoons dried chili peppers
25 g/1 oz lard	2 tablespoons lard

Dice the chicken. Mix half the cornflour and the egg in a bowl. Stir in the chicken. Mince the peanuts coarsely. Chop the spring onions into 1-cm/$\frac{1}{2}$-inch segments and combine with the remainder of the cornflour blended with the water, sugar, vinegar, soy sauce and salt in a bowl. Heat the oil to 180°C, 350°F, or until a day-old cube of bread turns golden in 1 minute. Deep-fry the diced chicken for 30 seconds. Drain and set aside. Remove and discard the chilli pepper seeds, chop and sauté in the lard for 30 seconds. Add the chicken and stir-fry for 10 seconds. Pour in the spring onion mixture and continue to stir-fry for 20 seconds. Sprinkle in the peanuts. After a few stirs, pour on to a heated serving dish.

NOTE   In the original recipe in Chinese, this dish is described as 'concurrently salty, sweet and aromatic and therefore highly palatable'.

Salt-buried chicken

Yen Kuo Chi

There are several versions of this unique manner of cooking chicken. This Cantonese method, which comes from the Pearl Dragon Dining Rooms, Chengtu, is probably the most elaborate.

Serve for a banquet or family meal

METRIC/IMPERIAL	AMERICAN
1 (900-g/2-lb) chicken	1 (2-lb) chicken
1 tablespoon soy sauce	1 tablespoon soy sauce
4 teaspoons chopped fresh root ginger	4 teaspoons chopped fresh ginger root
6 spring onions	6 scallions
1 teaspoon salt	1 teaspoon salt
2 tablespoons Rose Dew or cherry brandy	3 tablespoons Rose Dew or cherry brandy
2·75 kg/6 lb coarse grain salt	6 lb coarse grain salt (Kosher salt) may be substituted)
4 tablespoons secondary broth (see page 163)	$\frac{1}{3}$ cup secondary broth (see page 163)
Dip	*Dip*
2 tablespoons chopped spring onions	3 tablespoons chopped scallions
2 teaspoons chopped fresh root ginger	2 teaspoons chopped fresh ginger root
1 teaspoon salt	1 teaspoon salt
4 tablespoons secondary broth (see page 163)	$\frac{1}{3}$ cup secondary broth (see page 163)
2 teaspoons salad oil	2 teaspoons salad oil

Clean the chicken thoroughly and dip quickly in boiling water. Take out, pull and stretch. Dip in boiling water again. Dry the chicken thoroughly and rub the outside with the soy sauce. Hang up to dry for 3 hours.

Chop the ginger into small pieces. Wash the spring onions and crush them with the side of a knife, so that they are slightly bruised. Put the ginger and spring onions in a bowl and add the 1 teaspoon salt and the Rose Dew (a Chinese sweet liqueur) or cherry brandy. Mix them together. When the chicken is dry, stuff it with this mixture. Heat the coarse grain salt in a large cast iron pot. When quite hot, make a hole in the middle and bury the chicken. Cover the pot. Place it over low heat for 10 minutes. Remove from the heat and let stand for 10 minutes. Repeat this process twice more during the space of 1 hour. Alternatively, the cast iron pot can be placed in a preheated moderate oven (160°C, 325°F, Gas Mark 3) for $1\frac{1}{4}$ hours. Remove the chicken from the salt and chop the bird into $1\cdot5 \times 3$-cm/ $\frac{3}{4} \times 1\frac{1}{2}$-inch pieces. Remove and discard the stuffing.

Arrange the pieces of chicken on a heated plate in a spreadeagle pattern. Make the dip by boiling the spring onions, ginger, salt, secondary broth and salad oil together for 3-4 seconds. The diner usually dips the chicken in this mixture at the table before eating.

Quick-fried ribbon of duck

(Illustrated on pages 46-47)

Chiang Pao Ya Ssu

This is a dish which carries a highly savoury 'punch'. In all these quick-fried dishes, heat is supposed to carry and propel, in itself, a flavour of its own.

Serve for a banquet or family party

METRIC/IMPERIAL	AMERICAN
350 g/12 oz cooked or smoked duck	$\frac{3}{4}$ lb cooked or smoked duck
2-3 sticks celery	2-3 stalks celery
1 small leek	1 small leek
1 sweet red pepper	1 sweet red pepper
2 teaspoons dried chilli peppers	2 teaspoons dried chili peppers
2 cloves garlic	2 cloves garlic
50 g/2 oz lard	$\frac{1}{4}$ cup lard
1 tablespoon fermented black beans, soaked for 1 hour (see page 156)	1 tablespoon fermented black beans, soaked for 1 hour (see page 156)
1½ teaspoons castor sugar	1½ teaspoons sugar
1 tablespoon soy sauce	1 tablespoon soy sauce
1 tablespoon vinegar	1 tablespoon vinegar

Slice the duck into matchstick-thin strips. Trim the celery and leek and cut into similar-sized pieces. Remove and discard the seeds from the red pepper and chilli peppers. Cut into thin strips. Crush the garlic.

  Heat the lard in a frying pan. Sauté the chilli peppers in it for 1 minute to flavour the oil. Remove and discard the peppers. Add the celery, leek, garlic, sweet pepper and black beans. Stir-fry over high heat for 1 minute. Add the duck, sugar and soy sauce. Continue to stir-fry for 1 minute. Finally, add the vinegar and stir-fry quickly for 10 seconds.

Strange-flavour chicken

Kuai-Wei Chi K'uai

*The multiplicity of flavours present explains the name chosen for this dish.
It is a great favourite in Szechwan and is gaining popularity throughout
China.*

Serve for a banquet or family party

METRIC/IMPERIAL	AMERICAN
6-8 chicken drumsticks (about 675 g/1½ lb)	6-8 chicken drumsticks (about 1½ lb)
25 g/1 oz sesame seeds	3 tablespoons sesame seeds
1½ teaspoons sesame oil	1½ teaspoons sesame oil
1½ tablespoons soy sauce	2 tablespoons soy sauce
2 teaspoons castor sugar	2 teaspoons sugar
1 tablespoon vinegar	1 tablespoon vinegar
1 teaspoon chilli sauce	1 teaspoon chili sauce
¼ teaspoon freshly ground black pepper	¼ teaspoon freshly ground black pepper
6-8 spring onions	6-8 scallions

Cook the drumsticks in boiling water to cover for 20 minutes, allowing
5 minutes boiling and 15 minutes simmering time. Drain and cool for 10
minutes. Remove the meat from the drumsticks and slice each piece
diagonally into four pieces.

Stir-fry the sesame seeds gently in a dry pan over very low heat until they
are just turning golden and beginning to crackle. Place a third of these
seeds in a dry bowl and pound the remaining two-thirds to a powder in a
mortar, adding the sesame oil to make sesame paste. Mix this paste with the
soy sauce, sugar, vinegar, chilli sauce and pepper.

Chop the white parts of the spring onions (reserving the green parts for
use in another dish) and pile them in the centre of a heated serving dish.

Arrange the pieces of chicken around the edge by overlapping them,
skin-side up. Pour the sesame paste mixture evenly over the chicken and
sprinkle the crispy, dry sesame seeds on top before serving.

NOTE   The various flavours present (saltiness, sweetness, sourness and
hotness) give this dish a strong, aromatic appeal. It is quite often seen at
dinner tables in other parts of China, perhaps because it is different from
the usual Chinese chicken dishes.

Chicken gold-coin pagoda

Ching Ch'ien Chi Ta

This is another example of the Chinese addiction to fanciful names. The 'pagodas' here are, in fact, no more than piled-up canapés garnished with chopped ham, with a pork fat or bacon base. However, as it is considered one of the 'eight famous Szechwan dishes', it is worth trying. Its comparative simplicity should make the attempt rewarding.

Serve for a banquet

METRIC/IMPERIAL	AMERICAN
1 large breast of chicken	1 large chicken breast
3 tablespoons water	$\frac{1}{4}$ cup water
50 g/2 oz pork fat	$\frac{1}{4}$ cup fat back
4 eggs	4 eggs
$\frac{1}{2}$ teaspoon salt	$\frac{1}{2}$ teaspoon salt
6 rashers of thinly-sliced bacon	6 Canadian-style bacon slices
15 g/$\frac{1}{2}$ oz cornflour	2 tablespoons cornstarch
25 g/1 oz cooked smoked ham	1 thin slice cooked smoked ham
1 medium cucumber	1 medium cucumber
1 teaspoon castor sugar	1 teaspoon sugar
1$\frac{1}{2}$ teaspoons vinegar	1$\frac{1}{2}$ teaspoons vinegar
1 tablespoon light-coloured soy sauce	1 tablespoon light-colored soy sauce
1 teaspoon sesame oil	1 teaspoon sesame oil

Remove the flesh from the bone and mince the chicken. Place in a bowl, add half the water and beat 100 times in a clockwise direction. Mince the pork fat and add to the chicken together with 2 eggs. Beat in the same direction another 100 times. Add the salt and beat 50 times. Add the remaining water and beat another 50 times, always in the same direction.

Cut each rasher of bacon into four pieces. Mix the remaining eggs with the cornflour and brush each bacon piece with this batter. Spoon a portion of chicken on each piece of bacon. Using wet fingers, form into a round, flat shape. Chop the ham finely and use to garnish the top of each piece. Cut the cucumber into 6-cm/2$\frac{1}{2}$-inch lengths. Remove the peel in 1-cm/$\frac{1}{2}$-inch wide strips and retain for garnishing. Use a very sharp knife to slice the firm outside wall of the white part of cucumber into paper-thin 1-cm/$\frac{1}{2}$-inch wide slices. Discard the inner and softer parts of the cucumber. Marinate the cucumber slices for 15 minutes in sugar, vinegar, soy sauce and sesame oil.

Grease a large baking tray and arrange the 24 bacon pieces on it. Place the tray in a preheated moderately hot oven (190°C, 375°F, Gas Mark 5) for 10 minutes. Raise the heat to moderately hot (200°C, 400°F, Gas Mark 6) for a further 7-8 minutes, or until the 'gold coins' are quite crispy. Pile the 'gold coins' in the centre of a large, round, heated plate, forming them into a pyramid or 'pagoda' shape. Alternate the green and white cucumber strips so that they radiate from the centre, making the 'pagoda' the sun, and the cucumber strips the beams.

Double-cooked steamed pork with pickled salted cabbage

(Illustrated on page 45)

Shao Pai

This pork dish is cooked in the reverse order of the usual Double-cooked pork, *which is boiled first and fried afterwards. In this case, the pork is deep-fried first and steamed afterwards, adding ingredients and seasonings between the processes.*

Serve for a family meal

METRIC/IMPERIAL	AMERICAN
vegetable oil for deep-frying	vegetable oil for deep-frying
1 (675-g/1½-lb) piece belly of pork	1 (1½-lb) piece salt pork
1½ tablespoons sweet sherry	2 tablespoons sweet sherry
1 tablespoon soy sauce	1 tablespoon soy sauce
freshly ground black pepper	freshly ground black pepper
175 g/6 oz pickled Szechwan cabbage (see page 162)	1½ cups pickled Szechwan cabbage (see page 162)

Heat the oil to 180°C, 350°F, or until a day-old cube of bread turns golden in 1 minute. Deep-fry the pork for 10 minutes. Drain, cool and cut into 2·5 × 5-cm/1 × 2-inch slices, each piece containing both lean meat and fat. Arrange the pieces on a plate and add the sherry, soy sauce and pepper to taste. Marinate for 10 minutes. Arrange the pork in neat layers in a large ovenproof bowl. Chop the cabbage and place over the pork. Cover and steam for 40 minutes. Serve with rice.

Right *Steamed rice-pork 'pearls' (see page 81).*
Overleaf *Steamed beef in ground rice (see page 72); Soy-braised fish (see page 73); Quick-fried chicken (see page 74).*

T'ung Ching vegetarian noodles

(Illustrated on pages 46-47)

T'ung Ching Hsiang Su-Mien

This style of vegetarian noodles is an established dish in the Szechwan tradition. Originally, it was a popular dish of the masses, who often prepared it to entertain their friends and relatives on special occasions. It was also served from mobile carrier-stalls which were carried on shoulder-poles, with a charcoal cooker and washbasin at one end and the bowls, utensils, chopsticks and spoons at the other.

Serve as a snack

METRIC/IMPERIAL	AMERICAN
3 tablespoons sesame paste (see page 163)	$\frac{1}{4}$ cup sesame paste (see page 163)
1 tablespoon sesame oil	1 tablespoon sesame oil
2 tablespoons wine vinegar	3 tablespoons wine vinegar
1 teaspoon monosodium glutamate (optional)	1 teaspoon monosodium glutamate (optional)
1 tablespoon castor sugar	1 tablespoon sugar
2 tablespoons soy sauce	3 tablespoons soy sauce
1 teaspoon chilli sauce	1 teaspoon chili sauce
freshly ground black pepper	freshly ground black pepper
450 g/1 lb Chinese noodles (or spaghetti)	1 lb Chinese noodles (or spaghetti)
2 tablespoons finely chopped spring onion tops	3 tablespoons finely chopped scallion stems
1 tablespoon finely chopped garlic	1 tablespoon finely chopped garlic

Mix together the sesame paste, sesame oil, vinegar, monosodium glutamate, sugar, soy sauce, chilli sauce and pepper to taste. Divide the mixture among five separate bowls.

Boil the noodles or spaghetti for 15-20 minutes. Drain and while steaming hot, divide into five equal portions and place on top of the mixture in the five bowls. Sprinkle the noodles with the chopped spring onion tops and garlic. Each diner uses his own chopsticks to toss and mix the noodles or spaghetti with the ingredients and seasonings.

This is an extremely satisfying dish and should add a new dimension to vegetarian food.

Left Salt pork with cabbage heart (see page 103).

69

Mid-Yangtze

The Mid-Yangtze region has sometimes been called the Rice Bowl of China, since the three provinces I have included in this region, Hupeh, Hunan and Kiangsi, are rice-producing areas. It is also known as the Great Lake region of China. Although these large pools of water, acting as natural reservoirs for the Yangtze, are nothing compared with the Great Lakes of North America, they are fresh water and large by Chinese standards. The Tunting Lake in Hunan reaches 75 miles in length and 55 miles in width during the summer. The Poyang Lake in Kiangsi grows to 85 miles long and 20 miles wide. The combined population of the three provinces exceeds 72 million.

Apart from developing rice, tea, coal and tungsten, Kiangsi province has produced some of the most exquisite porcelains in China. It is from the small town of Ching Teh Cheng in Kiangsi that the bulk of the finest china in the world has come. The products of this small, remote town are those which, over the centuries, have stocked the great stately homes of Britain, France and other countries. Today, this china is fetching fabulous prices in the famous auction rooms of the world.

During the Taiping Rebellion of the mid-19th century, the Manchu Dynasty, with the help of General Gordon, recruited the bulk of the mercenaries from Hunan to suppress the rebellion. The people of this region are tough and renowned as fighters. They like their food hot; you will notice chilli being used in almost every other dish.

Wu-han (or the twin cities of Wuchang and Hankow), the capital of Hupeh, the third province, is the largest metropolis of the region. It is situated at the crossroads between the east-west communication along the Yangtze and the north-south communication along the Peking-Canton railway. It is gradually developing into one of the most important industrial complexes in the country. It was at Wu-han that the only bridge to span the Yangtze —a double-decker—was opened with great pride some years ago. The whole area, being the geographical centre of China, appears to have been so heavily awash in political turmoil and warfare during the past half-century or more that there seems to have been few establishments of permanence where culinary art could develop and prosper. Otherwise, the size of the area and of its population would lead one to expect a much greater culinary output.

As it is, dishes of character and individuality produced in this area are definitely more limited than those of any of the other areas of corresponding size and population.

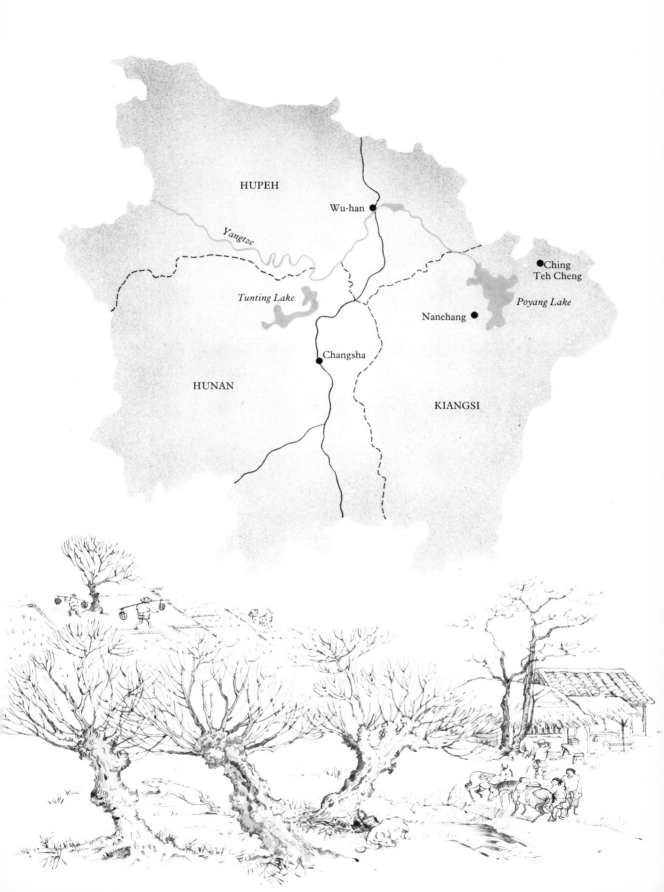

Steamed beef in ground rice

(Illustrated on pages 66-67)

Feng Cheng Niu Jou

In all other parts of China, pork is usually served with ground rice. In Szechwan, beef is used. Ground rice with meat gives an aromatic flavour.

Serve for a family meal

METRIC/IMPERIAL	AMERICAN
1 (800-g/1¾-lb) fillet or rump steak	1 (1¾-lb) beef tenderloin
1 tablespoon chopped fresh root ginger	1 tablespoon chopped fresh ginger root
5 tablespoons water	6 tablespoons water
1½ tablespoons vegetable oil	2 tablespoons vegetable oil
1 tablespoon dry sherry	1 tablespoon dry sherry
1½ tablespoons soy sauce	2 tablespoons soy sauce
1 tablespoon fermented black beans, soaked for 1 hour (see page 156)	1 tablespoon fermented black beans, soaked for 1 hour (see page 156)
1½ teaspoons castor sugar	1½ teaspoons sugar
1 teaspoon chilli sauce	1 teaspoon chili sauce
100 g/4 oz ground rice or semolina	1 cup medium to coarsely ground rice or semolina flour
crushed coriander seeds	crushed coriander seeds
bay leaves	bay leaves
chopped chives	chopped chives
fresh thyme	fresh thyme

Cut the meat into $1 \times 1 \cdot 5 \times 3$-cm/$\frac{1}{2} \times \frac{3}{4} \times 1\frac{1}{2}$-inch pieces. Prepare the ginger water by boiling the ginger in the water over low heat for 3 minutes, then strain. Place the meat in a bowl and add the ginger water, oil, sherry, soy sauce, black beans, sugar and chilli sauce. Work the mixture into the meat with your fingers. Finally, in a frying pan, dry-fry the ground rice stirring continuously until it begins to turn brown. Allow to cool, then use to coat the pieces of meat.

Divide the meat between four ovenproof bowls. To the first bowl, add a few coriander seeds, to the second, add a few bay leaves, to the third, add a few chives, and to the fourth, add a little thyme. Place the four bowls in a steamer, cover and steam for 30 minutes.

The beef in four flavours makes an excellent meal if served with rice and accompanied by a soup, a fish or egg dish and a vegetable dish.

Soy-braised fish

(Illustrated on pages 66-67)

Huang Men Yü

This is the traditional way of cooking fish in China, but the further one travels up the Yangtze, the less sugar is found in the recipe until it disappears entirely from the ingredients. It is the down-river people who are fond of sweet dishes.

Serve for a family meal

METRIC/IMPERIAL	AMERICAN
675 g/1½ lb fish fillets (bream, bass, carp, halibut or cod)	1½ lb fish fillets (bass, carp, halibut or cod)
1 teaspoon salt	1 teaspoon salt
4 spring onions	4 scallions
vegetable oil for deep-frying	vegetable oil for deep-frying
25 g/1 oz lard	2 tablespoons lard
4 slices fresh root ginger	4 slices fresh ginger root
1 teaspoon chilli powder	1 teaspoon chili powder
1 tablespoon soy sauce	1 tablespoon soy sauce
2 tablespoons dry sherry	3 tablespoons dry sherry
½ teaspoon monosodium glutamate (optional)	½ teaspoon monosodium glutamate (optional)
1 teaspoon sesame oil	1 teaspoon sesame oil

Chop the fish into approximately 2·5-cm/1-inch cubes. Rub evenly with the salt, using your fingers. Cut the spring onions into 2·5-cm/1-inch long pieces. Heat the oil to 180°C, 350°F, or until a day-old cube of bread turns golden in 1 minute, and deep-fry the fish for 2 minutes. Drain. Heat the lard in a frying pan and sauté the ginger and chilli powder for 30 seconds. Add the fish and turn it over in the lard a couple of times. Pour in the soy sauce and sherry. Turn the fish over several times and cover the pan. Simmer the contents over low heat for 3 minutes. Remove the lid and sprinkle the fish with the monosodium glutamate and sesame oil. Add the spring onions. Bring to the table on a heated serving dish.

NOTE   This is very much a household recipe. Traditionally, many people prefer fish fried this way without the use of batter. Because the gravy is sufficiently strong, no sauce-dips are required. Cooking the fish rapidly makes it white, juicy and succulent, contrasting in colour with the dark sauce.

Quick-fried chicken

(Illustrated on pages 66-67)

Wen Shan Chi T'ing

This is another dish of successfully contrasting textures. The sweet pepper and chilli peppers give the chicken a delicious piquant flavour.

Serve for a banquet or family meal

METRIC/IMPERIAL	AMERICAN
2 large breasts of chicken	2 large chicken breasts
50 g/2 oz bamboo shoots	$\frac{1}{2}$ cup bamboo shoots
1 small sweet red pepper	1 small sweet red pepper
1 spring onion	1 scallion
$\frac{1}{2}$ tablespoon dried chilli peppers	$1\frac{1}{2}$ teaspoons dried chili peppers
1 teaspoon salt	1 teaspoon salt
1 egg	1 egg
1 tablespoon cornflour	1 tablespoon cornstarch
3 tablespoons vegetable oil	$\frac{1}{4}$ cup vegetable oil
25 g/1 oz lard	2 tablespoons lard
4 tablespoons chicken broth	$\frac{1}{3}$ cup chicken broth
1 tablespoon dry sherry	1 tablespoon dry sherry
$\frac{1}{2}$ teaspoon monosodium glutamate (optional)	$\frac{1}{2}$ teaspoon monosodium glutamate (optional)
1 tablespoon light-coloured soy sauce	1 tablespoon light-colored soy sauce
1 teaspoon sesame oil	1 teaspoon sesame oil

Cut the breasts of chicken into 5-mm/$\frac{1}{4}$-inch cubes. Cut the bamboo shoots and the trimmed and deseeded sweet pepper into similar-sized pieces. Slice the spring onion into 5-mm/$\frac{1}{4}$-inch pieces. Chop the chilli peppers and discard the seeds.

Place the diced chicken in a bowl. Add the salt and rub it into the chicken. Break the egg into a bowl and mix well. Then whisk in the cornflour until smooth. Heat the vegetable oil in a large frying pan. When quite hot, coat the chicken in the cornflour mixture and stir-fry for $1\frac{1}{2}$ minutes. Remove the chicken and discard any remaining oil. Add the lard to the pan. Stir-fry the bamboo shoots, sweet red pepper and the chilli peppers over high heat for 2 minutes. Mix the chicken broth with the sherry and add together with the monosodium glutamate, soy sauce and sesame oil. Stir-fry gently for 30 seconds. Add the pieces of chicken and continue to stir-fry for another 30 seconds. Transfer to a heated dish and serve.

Toss-fried rice noodles

Ch'ao Mi Fen

The frying of noodles in lard and meat juice gives them a savoury 'lubricant' which is very appealing to lovers of pasta. The use of crunchy textures such as bamboo shoots and celery, soft materials like mushrooms and noodles, and strong-tasting and aromatic ingredients such as leeks and garlic, as in this recipe, creates an interesting contrast in texture, aroma and taste.

Serve for a family meal or snack

METRIC/IMPERIAL	AMERICAN
675 g/1½ lb rice stick noodles (see page 158)	1½ lb rice stick noodles (see page 158)
225 g/8 oz lean pork	½ lb lean pork
40 g/1½ oz dried Chinese mushrooms, soaked and drained	1½ cup dried Chinese mushrooms, soaked and drained
50 g/2 oz bamboo shoots	½ cup bamboo shoots
½ stick celery	½ stalk celery
1 small leek	1 small leek
2 cloves garlic	2 cloves garlic
50 g/2 oz lard	¼ cup lard
2 tablespoons soy sauce	3 tablespoons soy sauce
150 ml/¼ pint chicken or superior broth (see page 170)	⅔ cup chicken or superior broth (see page 170)
1 teaspoon monosodium glutamate (optional)	1 teaspoon monosodium glutamate (optional)

Place the noodles in a pan of boiling water and boil gently until soft and cooked (this should be about 5-10 minutes). Drain and cool under cold running water, then set aside.

Slice the pork, mushrooms, bamboo shoots, celery and leek into matchstick-thin strips. Crush the garlic.

Heat three-quarters of the lard in a frying pan over high heat. Add the pork and bamboo shoots; stir-fry for 30 seconds and then add the mushrooms, the leek and garlic. Fry for 1 minute. Add the celery, soy sauce, broth and monosodium glutamate. Simmer for 2 minutes. Remove from the heat and place the contents of the pan in a bowl.

Add the remainder of the lard to the frying pan. Place over medium heat for 30 seconds. Then add the cooked noodles. Stir-fry gently for 3 minutes. Add half the pork mixture and all its liquid. Continue to stir-fry for 2 minutes. By this time, the noodles should have absorbed all the liquid. Turn the contents on to a large, flat, heated serving dish. Heat the remainder of the pork mixture in the pan over high heat for 1 minute and use it as a hot garnish or topping for the noodles.

NOTE For ultimate enjoyment and appreciation, this dish should be eaten hot and without accompaniment.

North Yangtze

The area north of the Yangtze is very much tougher than the areas south of the river. Most of the rougher manual work in the South-of-the-River areas seems to be performed by men who have migrated to find work in the larger towns and cities. An old-style warlord general, General Tang Tzu Chang, one of the defenders of Shanghai during the Sino-Japanese War (who later became a professional artist and actually did a number of designs for an art publishing firm I was running), was the commanding general in the Hsuchow area during his earlier marauding warlord days. He once told me that every second person in the area was an outlaw.

Although northern Kiangsu and the province of Anhwei (which has an area of approximately 54 thousand square miles and a population of over 33 million) were important rice producing regions, the fact that they were situated between the Yellow River and the Yangtze meant that they were very much affected by drought and flood. It is natural that the inhabitants of the area saw days of both comparative affluence and downright famine.

Historically, the area has produced, apart from hordes of outlaws and refugees, a good sprinkling of cultivated politicians and men of letters. Since outlaws and refugees do not often account for excellence in cuisine, it was probably these small groups of cultured and cultivated people who were responsible for some of the surprisingly well-devised and delicate dishes which are produced and eaten in towns like Yangchow and Hofei.

As one travels northwards after crossing the Yangtze at Nanking, the Pukow-Tientsin stretch of the railway, from Shanghai to Peking, runs through several hundred miles of featureless plains. The region is perhaps like the areas around Leicester in England, or, on a larger scale, the American Middle West. This area is, in fact, the southern reaches of the Central Plain of North China. When the harvest is good, Wu-Hu, the port on the Yangtze, is one of the greatest rice-marketing centres of China; and the grain merchants are a wealthy class of people.

Plentiful grain cereals in good years must have accounted for the wide availability of poultry and swine, which are well represented in the diet of the region, together with a wide range of fresh vegetables. The use of lamb and mutton is a practice which originated in the north. This is certainly an area which overlaps both north and south. A number of the recipes I have chosen to represent the region should give a clue to the inevitable influence of geography on the food and culinary habits of the people.

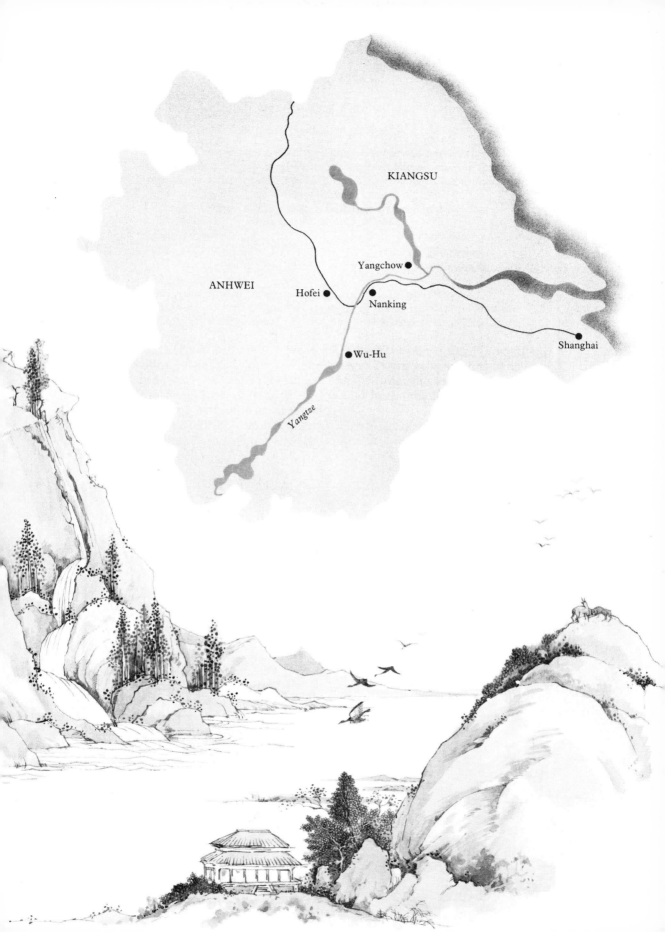

KIANGSU

ANHWEI

Yangchow ●

Hofei ● ● Nanking

●Wu-Hu

● Shanghai

Yangtze

Meat-filled mushrooms

(Illustrated on pages 86-87)

Hsiang Ku Ho

This recipe comes from Chef Pei Hsiung Pan of Hofei, Anhwei. It is a dainty and very savoury introductory dish for a multi-course dinner.

Serve for a banquet

METRIC/IMPERIAL	AMERICAN
30 large dried Chinese mushrooms	30 large dried Chinese mushrooms
100 g/4 oz lean pork	$\frac{1}{4}$ lb lean pork
25 g/1 oz cooked smoked ham	2 tablespoons cooked smoked ham
1 egg	1 egg
1 tablespoon chopped onion	1 tablespoon chopped onion
1 tablespoon ground dried shrimps	1 tablespoon ground dried shrimps
1 tablespoon cornflour	1 tablespoon cornstarch
1 tablespoon soy sauce	1 tablespoon soy sauce
$\frac{1}{2}$ teaspoon salt	$\frac{1}{2}$ teaspoon salt
Sauce	*Sauce*
150 ml/$\frac{1}{4}$ pint chicken broth	$\frac{2}{3}$ cup chicken broth
2 teaspoons cornflour	2 teaspoons cornstarch
$\frac{1}{2}$ teaspoon monosodium glutamate (optional)	$\frac{1}{2}$ teaspoon monosodium glutamate (optional)
15 g/$\frac{1}{2}$ oz lard	$1\frac{1}{2}$ teaspoons lard

Remove the stalks from the mushrooms. Soak the mushroom caps in warm water for 30 minutes. Mince the pork and ham and mix in a bowl with the egg, onion, shrimps, cornflour, half the soy sauce and half the salt. Spread the mixture over the inside of 15 of the mushroom caps and cover each one with a second mushroom cap. Put a board over them and press gently to flatten, keeping the insides of the caps together, sandwich-style.

Arrange these 'sandwiches' on a suitable plate and place in a steamer. Cover and steam for 20 minutes. Meanwhile, prepare a sauce by mixing the remaining soy sauce and salt with the broth, cornflour and monosodium glutamate. Heat gently, stirring continuously until thickened, bring to the boil and add the lard.

Pour the sauce over the mushrooms and serve immediately.

Fry-braised fish balls

(Illustrated on pages 86-87)

Ch'ao Hun Yü Ku

This dish is very popular in Kwangsi homes. It is a recipe used by many well-known chefs in Nanking.

Serve for a family meal or party

METRIC/IMPERIAL	AMERICAN
1 (900-g/2-lb) white fish (carp, cod, haddock, bass or halibut)	1 (2-lb) white fish (carp, cod, haddock, bass or halibut)
1 egg	1 egg
1½ teaspoons salt	1½ teaspoons salt
½ teaspoon monosodium glutamate (optional)	½ teaspoon monosodium glutamate (optional)
2 teaspoons sesame oil	2 teaspoons sesame oil
freshly ground black pepper	freshly ground black pepper
2 tablespoons water	3 tablespoons water
½ small sweet green pepper	½ small sweet green pepper
3 water chestnuts	3 water chestnuts
8 dried Chinese mushrooms, soaked and drained	8 dried Chinese mushrooms, soaked and drained
2 cloves garlic	2 cloves garlic
vegetable oil for deep-frying	vegetable oil for deep-frying
3 tablespoons vegetable oil	¼ cup vegetable oil
25 g/1 oz bean sprouts	⅓ cup bean sprouts
3 slices fresh root ginger	3 slices fresh ginger root
1 tablespoon chutney	1 tablespoon chutney
3 tablespoons superior broth (see page 170)	¼ cup superior broth (see page 170)
15 g/½ oz cornflour	2 tablespoons cornstarch

Clean the fish, fillet it and mince the flesh. Beat the egg and add together with 1 teaspoon of the salt, the monosodium glutamate, half the sesame oil, pepper to taste and the water. Beat well. Form into balls about 1 cm/½ inch in diameter. Thinly slice the green pepper and water chestnuts. Remove and discard the mushroom stalks. Slice the garlic.

Heat the oil for deep-frying to 180°C, 350°F, or until a day-old cube of bread turns golden in 1 minute. Deep-fry the fish balls for 2 minutes, until lightly browned. Drain and simmer in boiling water for 2 minutes. Drain and set aside.

Place the 3 tablespoons (U.S. ¼ cup) oil in a large frying pan. Place over high heat for 30 seconds. Add the remaining salt, the green pepper, water chestnuts, mushrooms, garlic, bean sprouts, ginger and chutney. Stir-fry quickly for 2 minutes. Add the fish balls and continue to stir-fry more slowly over lower heat for 1 minute. Add the broth and cornflour blended with a little water. Stir for 10 seconds and sprinkle with the remaining sesame oil. Serve immediately.

Sliced sole
in braised hearts of spring greens

(Illustrated on pages 86-87)

Sha Yu T'sai T'ai

It is seldom that fish and spring greens form the main ingredients of a dish. In this recipe, the white of the fish and the green of the vegetable make for an attractive colour combination, and the natural softness of both provides an interesting contrast in texture to accompanying dishes.

Serve for a banquet or family meal

METRIC/IMPERIAL	AMERICAN
675 g/1½ lb fillets of sole	1½ lb fillets of sole
1 teaspoon salt	1 teaspoon salt
2 teaspoons cornflour	2 teaspoons cornstarch
1 egg white	1 egg white
1·25 kg/2½ lb celery cabbage	2 medium heads of lettuce or
40 g/1½ oz bamboo shoots	young cabbage
40 g/1½ oz lard	½ cup bamboo shoots
150 ml/¼ pint chicken broth	3 tablespoons lard
¾ teaspoon monosodium glutamate	⅔ cup chicken broth
(optional)	¾ teaspoon monosodium glutamate
freshly ground black pepper	(optional)
	freshly ground black pepper

Cut the fish fillets into 2·5 × 5-cm/1 × 2-inch pieces. Mix half the salt with the cornflour and egg white to form a batter. Coat the fish with this batter. Remove and discard all the outer leaves of the spring greens, leaving only the hearts. Cut each heart into quarters and again into 5-cm/2-inch lengths. Thinly slice the bamboo shoots.

  Heat the lard in a frying pan. Add the pieces of fish and sauté for 1 minute on each side. Remove and drain. Add the spring greens to the pan and sauté for 2 minutes. Then add the remaining salt, the bamboo shoots and chicken broth. Simmer for 5 minutes. Return the fish to the pan. Cover and simmer for 2 minutes. Sprinkle with the monosodium glutamate and pepper to taste. Arrange the spring greens on a heated plate with the pieces of fish as neatly as possible on top and serve immediately.

  This is a pleasant dish rather than a strong-tasting one. Since Chinese cooking abounds in well-seasoned and delicious dishes, the simple freshness of this one makes for a good contrast.

Steamed rice-pork 'pearls'

(Illustrated on page 65)

Cheng Mi Fen Yüan Tzu

The areas around the Tunting Lake produce a breed of pig, the flesh of which is noted for its tenderness. The best glutinous rice comes from the Liu Yang county of Hunan. It is from these two basic materials that this recipe is created.

Serve for a family meal or party

METRIC/IMPERIAL	AMERICAN
225 g/8 oz short-grain rice	1 cup short-grain rice
575 g/1¼ lb lean pork	1¼ lb lean pork
350 g/12 oz pork fat	¾ lb fat back
8 water chestnuts	8 water chestnuts
2 teaspoons salt	2 teaspoons salt
¼ teaspoon freshly ground black pepper	¼ teaspoon freshly ground black pepper
1 teaspoon monosodium glutamate (optional)	1 teaspoon monosodium glutamate (optional)
3 eggs	3 eggs
1 tablespoon dry sherry	1 tablespoon dry sherry
1½ tablespoons cornflour	2 tablespoons cornstarch
5 tablespoons water	6 tablespoons water
4 spring onions, chopped	4 scallions, chopped
2 teaspoons chopped fresh ginger root	2 teaspoons chopped fresh root ginger

Wash the rice three times and soak in cold water for 1 hour. Drain well and spread on a tray or sheet of greaseproof paper. Mince the lean pork. Boil the pork fat in water for 5 minutes, drain and cut into pea-sized pieces. Cut the water chestnuts into pieces of the same size.

Place the pork in a bowl and add the salt, pepper, monosodium glutamate, eggs, sherry and cornflour blended with the water. Mix well. Then add the pork fat, water chestnuts, spring onions and ginger. Use your hands to form the mixture into meatballs, 1 cm/½ inch in diameter. Roll them in the rice to pick up a covering of grains. When well-covered, use your hands to press the rice more firmly into the meatballs.

Arrange the rice-covered meatballs in not more than two layers in a large ovenproof dish. Cover with foil and steam vigorously for 20 minutes. These rice-pork 'pearls', being white, are best served in a solid-colour serving dish and should be brought to the table. They are best eaten dipped in soy sauce.

Although rice is the principal accompaniment to most Chinese meals, the abundance of it in this region results in its incorporation into savoury meat dishes.

East China

In Chinese history and literature, this area is referred to in essays and novels as East-of-the-River or sometimes South-of-the-River. Geographically, it is really the south bank of the Yangtze River delta. The principal cities are Nanking (several times capital of China), Soochow, Shanghai (the largest city in China, with a population of over 7 million) and Hangchow. Fortunately, only the area immediately bordering the river consists of mudflats, and the delta soon gives way to the fairly hilly areas to the south, making the region more picturesque and interesting than it would be otherwise.

In contrast to the arid barrenness of the north with its piercing winter wind, the climate and life South-of-the-River are supposed to be much milder and easier. In fact, the winter is quite cold in the Yangtze River valley, even in its lower reaches, and the summer swelteringly hot. But both the spring and autumn here are beautiful. The spring is unmarred by the drought and dust-storms of the north. The warm sun is balanced by occasional drizzle and misty rain. And the autumn, like everywhere else in China, is one of long, windless sunshine. The men of letters here talked and wrote about flowers, reunions, brilliant conversations, boating banquets and houseboats with concubines. All this creates an atmosphere of good living and good eating. Yet life here is not over-refined. For this is also an area of many talents and tremendous enterprise.

As I remember it, Shanghai was a cross between Chicago and the Berlin of the Weimar Republic. It was a city brimful of sin, partly ruled by the Municipal Council of the International Concessions and the Japanese gunboats, partly by the local gangsters and government officers, all trying to ride out the mounting tide of the Chinese Revolution. It is now principally an industrial centre, destined to be one of the largest manufacturing cities in the world.

Soochow, a mulberry-covered, silk-producing city, is reputed to produce the prettiest girls in China. They have light, smooth skins and extremely delicate bones and features.

The Grand Canal winds from Hangchow to Peking, some thousand miles away to the north. The whole area is criss-crossed with streams, canals and rivers. It is little wonder that the people here eat a wide variety of freshwater fish, crabs, shrimps and prawns. Shanghai, being a metropolitan city like Peking, boasts the dishes of China. The yellow rice wine produced in the city of Shao Hsing is one of the best known in China.

Shao Hsing Soup

(Illustrated on pages 106-107)

Shao Hsing T'ang

This is a simple soup using the products of the locality, devised by the Shanghai Municipal Catering Company. Here, the locally caught river shrimps are used and they are not peeled before cooking. In the West, it is best to shell the shrimps first.

Serve for a family meal or party

METRIC/IMPERIAL	AMERICAN
40 g/1½ oz bamboo shoots	2 bamboo shoots
½ bunch watercress	½ bunch watercress
½ small cucumber	½ small cucumber
600 ml/1 pint superior broth (see page 170)	2½ cups superior broth (see page 170)
100 g/4 oz cooked, peeled shrimps	¼ lb cooked, shelled shrimp
1½ teaspoons salt	1½ teaspoons salt
15 g/½ oz lard	1 tablespoon lard
2 tablespoons Shao Hsing wine or dry sherry	3 tablespoons Shao Hsing wine or dry sherry
1 teaspoon monosodium glutamate (optional)	1 teaspoon monosodium glutamate (optional)

Cut the bamboo shoots into pieces shaped like a triangular axe head. Clean the watercress thoroughly and remove the stalks. Cut the unpeeled cucumber into the same-sized triangular pieces as the bamboo shoots.

Bring the broth to the boil in a saucepan. Add the bamboo shoots. After 1 minute, add the cucumber, followed by the watercress, shrimps and salt. Lower the heat and simmer for 1 minute. Add the lard, Shao Hsing wine (or dry sherry) and monosodium glutamate. Pour into a large heated soup bowl or tureen. As the total cooking time does not exceed 3 minutes, there is a freshness about all the ingredients. The lard provides the smoothness; the wine and monosodium glutamate provide that 'pick-me-up' quality. Once again, here is a simple recipe with a connoisseur's appeal.

Right *Tung-Po pork (see page 91).*
Overleaf *Sliced sole in brasied hearts of spring greens (see page 80); Meat-filled mushrooms (see page 78); Fry-braised fish balls (see page 79).*

Vegetable rice

T'sai Fan

This recipe, from the Mei Yee Chai Restaurant, Shanghai, is included because it is so characteristic of the region. It is such a plain and simple dish that much more savoury food is usually eaten with it.

Serve for a family meal

METRIC/IMPERIAL	AMERICAN
675 g/1½ lb long-grain rice	3½ cups long-grain rice
675 g/1½ lb spring greens	1 medium head cabbage
25 g/1 oz lard	2 tablespoons lard
2 teaspoons salt	2 teaspoons salt
600 ml/1 pint cold water	2½ cups cold water
150 ml/¼ pint boiling water	⅔ cup boiling water

Wash the rice and let it soak in cold water for 3 hours. Clean the spring greens thoroughly; remove and discard the coarser outer leaves and stalks. Cut the remainder into 2·5-cm/1-inch squares.

Heat the lard in a large heavy saucepan. When it is very hot, add the spring greens. Reduce the heat and stir-fry gently for 3 minutes and then add the salt and the cold water. Turn up the heat. When the water starts to boil, add the rice. Continue to stir gently with a wooden spoon until the water reboils. Then lower the heat and cover tightly. After about 10-12 minutes, when the water has nearly all been absorbed by the rice, pour in the boiling water. Poke four holes through the rice to the bottom of the pan to facilitate steaming. Cover firmly and insert an asbestos mat underneath the pan. After 5 minutes, turn off the heat. Allow the rice to steam in its own heat for 10 minutes. The vegetable rice should then be ready.

NOTE Rice cooked with a vegetable in this manner is usually eaten with pickles or highly savoury food in order to make a well-balanced meal.

Left *Spare ribs and water chestnuts in thick gravy (see page 90).*

Spare ribs and water chestnuts in thick gravy

(Illustrated on page 88)

Ku Chiang Yü Ni

This dish is essentially for home cooking. It is not elegant enough for a feast or a banquet, but is extremely tasty all the same.

Serve for a family meal

METRIC/IMPERIAL	AMERICAN
675 g/1½ lb pork spare ribs	1½ lb spareribs
12 water chestnuts	12 water chestnuts
25 g/1 oz lard	2 tablespoons lard
1½ tablespoons chopped onion	2 tablespoons chopped onion
1 teaspoon chopped fresh root ginger	1 teaspoon chopped fresh ginger root
1½ tablespoons castor sugar	2 tablespoons sugar
2 tablespoons dry sherry	3 tablespoons dry sherry
2 tablespoons soy sauce	3 tablespoons soy sauce
150 ml/¼ pint water	⅔ cup water
6 tablespoons superior broth (see page 170)	½ cup superior broth (see page 170)
1 teaspoon monosodium glutamate (optional)	1 teaspoon monosodium glutamate (optional)
1 tablespoon cornflour	1 tablespoon cornstarch

Separate the spare ribs and chop them into 3-cm/1½-inch pieces. Cut the water chestnuts into quarters, if large, or halves if small. Fry the spare ribs in the lard for 5 to 6 minutes until they turn brown. Add the onion, ginger, sugar, half the sherry, half the soy sauce and finally the water. Cover and simmer gently for 30 minutes.

By this time there should be about 2 to 4 tablespoons of liquid left in the pan. Turn the heat to high and bring the contents to a rolling boil. Add the water chestnuts and broth. Stir the contents gently with a wooden spoon.

When the liquid is reduced to about half, add the remaining sherry and soy sauce, the monosodium glutamate and the cornflour mixed with 1 tablespoon of water. Stir gently for 30 to 40 seconds. Serve on a heated dish with plain boiled rice as an accompaniment.

Tung-Po pork

(Illustrated on page 85)

Tung-Po Jou

This is a very famous dish attributed to the poet Soo Tung-Po, the Robert Burns of China, who lived during the Sung Dynasty. This was one of the dishes with which he used to entertain his friends.

Serve for a family meal or party

METRIC/IMPERIAL	AMERICAN
1 (1·5-kg/3-lb) piece belly of pork (see recipe)	1 (3-lb) piece salt pork (see recipe)
2 tablespoons brown rock sugar (see page 163)	3 tablespoons brown rock sugar (see page 163)
4 tablespoons dry sherry	$\frac{1}{3}$ cup dry sherry
3 tablespoons soy sauce	$\frac{1}{4}$ cup soy sauce
2 medium onions	2 medium onions
4 large slices fresh root ginger	4 large slices fresh ginger root

Select a piece of pork with thin skin and with at least three layers of meat and fat, about 3 cm/$1\frac{1}{2}$ inches thick. Boil the pork in water to cover for 5 to 6 minutes. Drain and cut into four pieces, each piece with pork skin attached. Marinate the pieces of pork in the sugar, sherry and soy sauce for 30 minutes, turning them over three times.

Place a bamboo-frame (like a round mat, only three to four times thicker) at the bottom of a flameproof pot or heavy saucepan with a lid. The purpose of this is to prevent the meat from touching the bottom of the pan, where it might burn. Drain and arrange the pieces of pork on the frame, skin-side down. Cut the onions in quarters and place them with the ginger on top of each piece. Pour the marinade over the pork. Cover the pot or casserole as tightly as possible (in China it is sealed with dough). Place it over very low heat and cook gently for $2\frac{1}{4}$ hours.

Open the lid, transfer the pieces of pork to a clean ovenproof dish with a lid. Arrange three pieces of pork at the bottom of the dish with the remaining pieces on top, skin-side up. Skim the fat off the marinade, remove the ginger and onion and pour the marinade over the pork. Cover the ovenproof dish and steam for 10 to 15 minutes before serving.

NOTE For westerners, this could be a connoisseur's dish but it may take time to cultivate the taste for it. In a western kitchen, it might be easier to cook this dish in a casserole in a cool oven (150°C, 300°F, Gas Mark 2) for $2\frac{1}{2}$ hours. In this way, one can dispense with the bamboo frame.

Fried pork spare ribs

Yu Cha P'ai Ku

This highly spiced dish is ideal for eating with Vegetable rice *(see page 89). It calls for a cut of pork such as rib chops or spare ribs.*

Serve for a family meal

METRIC/IMPERIAL	AMERICAN
1·75 kg/4 lb pork spare ribs	4 lb pork spareribs
4 tablespoons soy sauce	$\frac{1}{3}$ cup soy sauce
2 tablespoons dry sherry	3 tablespoons dry sherry
1 tablespoon chopped fresh root ginger	1 tablespoon chopped fresh ginger root
1 tablespoon dried tangerine or orange peel (see page 159)	1 tablespoon dried tangerine or orange peel (see page 159)
1½ tablespoons castor sugar	2 tablespoons sugar
vegetable oil for deep-frying	vegetable oil for deep-frying
1 teaspoon chilli sauce	1 teaspoon chili sauce
$\frac{1}{4}$ teaspoon five-spice powder (see page 160)	$\frac{1}{4}$ teaspoon five-spice powder (see page 160)

Separate each spare rib and then chop into 6-cm/2½-inch lengths. Place in a bowl along with half the soy sauce, half the sherry, ginger, tangerine peel and sugar. Marinate for 1 hour. Drain the ribs and place in a wire basket. Heat the oil to 180°C, 350°F, or until a day-old cube of bread turns golden in 1 minute. Deep-fry the ribs for 2 to 2½ minutes until almost golden. Drain, place in a pan and pour in the remaining soy sauce and sherry, the chilli sauce and five-spice powder. Mix well and stir-fry for 15 seconds over high heat. Serve on a flat dish.

NOTE   The Chinese regard these ribs as miniature chops. Being thoroughly practised and dexterous in detaching meat from the bone in their mouths, they prefer these to larger chunks of meat.

Ham in honeyed sauce

Ping-T'ang Yüan T'i

This recipe comes from the Ta Hung Yun Restaurant, Shanghai, and although it is an acquired taste, it is also a memorable one. In a multi-course dinner, it is an excellent dish to break the monotony of ordinary fried savoury dishes.

Serve for a banquet

METRIC/IMPERIAL	AMERICAN
1 (1·5-1·75-kg/3-4-lb) hock smoked ham or gammon	1 (3-4-lb) smoked ham shank
50 g/2 oz lotus seeds	$\frac{1}{4}$ cup lotus seeds
50 g/2 oz brown rock sugar (see page 163)	$\frac{1}{3}$ cup brown rock sugar (see page 163)
3 tablespoons boiling water	$\frac{1}{4}$ cup boiling water
1$\frac{1}{2}$ tablespoons castor sugar	2 tablespoons sugar
1 tablespoon clear honey	1 tablespoon clear honey
1 tablespoon cornflour	1 tablespoon cornstarch

Soak the ham in water for several hours. Drain, place in a saucepan of cold water, bring to the boil and simmer for 2 hours. Remove the ham, make a deep incision in the side and take out the bone. Stuff the cavity with the lotus seeds and half the rock sugar. Place in a bowl. Cover and steam for 1 hour. Drain off excess moisture. Cut the piece of ham into 15 pieces. Place on a dish with the lotus seeds on top. Sprinkle with the remaining rock sugar. Place the dish in a steamer, cover and steam for a further 1 hour.

Drain the juices from the dish into a pan and add the boiling water, sugar and honey. Bring to the boil. Thicken with the cornflour blended with a little water and pour the sauce over the ham and lotus seeds before serving.

Red-simmered knuckle of pork

Mi Chih Huo Chung

This is essentially the standard Chinese red-cooked pork, except that more sugar is used. In spite of the liberal use of sugar, the meat tastes more savoury than sweet. Perhaps this is due to the counteracting effect of the equally large quantity of soy sauce.

Serve for a family meal

METRIC/IMPERIAL	AMERICAN
1 (1·5-1·75-kg/3-4-lb) knuckle of pork	1 (3-4-lb) pork hock
1·75 litres/3 pints water	$7\frac{1}{2}$ cups water
3 spring onions	3 scallions
6 tablespoons soy sauce	$\frac{1}{2}$ cup soy sauce
40 g/1½ oz castor sugar	$\frac{1}{4}$ cup sugar
6 tablespoons dry sherry	$\frac{1}{2}$ cup dry sherry
4 slices fresh root ginger	4 slices fresh ginger root
25 g/1 oz lard	2 tablespoons lard

Clean the knuckle of pork and slash with a knife on either side to facilitate cooking. Place in a heavy pan and add the water. Bring to the boil and simmer for 10 minutes. Skim and simmer for another 15 minutes. Skim again, ladle out and discard one-third of the broth. Cut the spring onions into 2·5-cm/1-inch segments. Add the spring onions, soy sauce, sugar, sherry, ginger and lard to the remaining broth. Cover and continue to simmer over low heat for 2 hours, uncovering once every 30 minutes to turn the knuckle over during cooking.

 By the end of 2 hours, the liquid in the pan should have reduced to a quarter. Reduce it again by half by increasing the heat for a few minutes. The gravy will have become rich brown and glossy. Lift out the knuckle of pork and place in a deep bowl. Pour the gravy over without any further thickening. For those who love rich food, there are few dishes in the world to surpass this pork. It is best eaten with plain, cooked vegetables and rice.

Butterfly bêche-de-mer

Hu T'ieh Hai Shen

Bêche-de-mer is a delicacy in China. It is eaten more for its texture than for its taste.

Serve for a banquet

METRIC/IMPERIAL	AMERICAN
1 (450-g/1-lb) bêche-de-mer, (see page 157)	1 (1-lb) bêche-de-mer, (see page 157)
2 eggs	2 eggs
1 slice cooked smoked ham	1 slice cooked smoked ham
25 g/1 oz cooked breast of chicken	½ cooked chicken breast
1 teaspoon cornflour	1 teaspoon cornstarch
½ teaspoon monosodium glutamate (optional)	½ teaspoon monosodium glutamate (optional)
2 tablespoons water	3 tablespoons water
1 tablespoon bean sprouts	1 tablespoon bean sprouts
225 g/8 oz knuckle of pork	½ lb pork hock
225 g/8 oz chicken	½ lb chicken
900 ml/1½ pints water	3¾ cups water
4 slices fresh root ginger	4 slices fresh ginger root
2 tablespoons dry sherry	3 tablespoons dry sherry
6 spring onions	6 scallions
25 g/1 oz lard	2 tablespoons lard
½ teaspoon salt	½ teaspoon salt

Scrub the bêche-de-mer gently with a hard brush to clean. Soak for 24 hours in warm water, changing the water several times. Clean carefully, remove the internal organs and then rinse in fresh water. Shape with a knife by cutting a 'V' in the centre leaving two 'wings' on either side. Dip in boiling water for 3 minutes and set aside. Hard-boil the eggs. Reserve the yolks for another dish and cut the whites into thin slices. Cut the ham and the cooked breast of chicken into 2·5-cm/1-inch long, thin, flat slices. Blend the cornflour and monosodium glutamate with 2 tablespoons of water and mix with the bean sprouts.

Make several slashes on the meat of the knuckle of pork. Blanch the knuckle and uncooked chicken in boiling water for 3 minutes. Drain and place them in a saucepan. Add the 900 ml/1½ pints (U.S. 3¾ cups) water, half the ginger, half the sherry and half the spring onions. Bring to the boil and simmer gently for 3 hours. Strain the broth and set aside.

Heat the lard in a frying pan. Add the remaining half of the ginger and spring onions. Sauté these for 2 minutes and then discard. Lower the bêche-de-mer gently into the hot lard and sauté for 1 minute. Turn over once and add the egg whites, ham, cooked chicken, remaining sherry, reserved broth and salt. Reduce the heat and simmer for 15 minutes. Add the bean sprout mixture. Bring to the boil and after 1 minute of simmering, serve in a large soup dish or tureen.

Soft-fried crabmeat

Ch'ao Hsia Fen

There is a local saying that 'after crab, nothing has any flavour' — which gives an idea of how much crab is prized as a delicacy in the region.

Serve for a banquet or family meal

METRIC/IMPERIAL	AMERICAN
450 g/1 lb fresh crabmeat	1 lb fresh crabmeat
2 tablespoons chopped onion	3 tablespoons chopped onion
3 tablespoons dry sherry	$\frac{1}{4}$ cup dry sherry
1 tablespoon cornflour	1 tablespoon cornstarch
2 tablespoons water	3 tablespoons water
25 g/1 oz pork fat	2 tablespoons fat back
40 g/1$\frac{1}{2}$ oz lard	3 tablespoons lard
$\frac{1}{4}$ teaspoon salt	$\frac{1}{4}$ teaspoon salt
1 tablespoon soy sauce	1 tablespoon soy sauce
1$\frac{1}{2}$ teaspoons castor sugar	1$\frac{1}{2}$ teaspoons sugar
4 tablespoons chicken broth	$\frac{1}{3}$ cup chicken broth
1$\frac{1}{2}$ tablespoons ginger water	2 tablespoons ginger water
(see page 160)	(see page 160)

Mix the crabmeat with half the onion and half the sherry. Blend the cornflour with the water. Cut the pork fat into small cubes.

Heat two-thirds of the lard in a frying pan. Add the remaining onion and pork fat and sauté until golden. Add the crabmeat mixture and stir-fry very gently without breaking it into pieces. After 30 seconds, add the remaining sherry, salt, soy sauce, sugar, chicken broth and ginger water. Mix gently and simmer for 3 minutes. Add the cornflour mixture and remaining lard. When it boils, the dish is ready. The usual dips used in China for this dish are mixtures of chopped root ginger with vinegar, or chopped garlic with vinegar.

Fried fish strips tossed in celery

Pan Yü Kua

This dish is in the Chinese tradition of the 'cooked salad' in which the crispy fish strips are mixed with crunchy celery and garnished with ham. An attractive dish which is most acceptable to the western palate.

Serve for a banquet or family meal

METRIC/IMPERIAL	AMERICAN
450 g/1 lb fish fillet	1 lb fish fillet
(bass, haddock, pike or cod)	(bass, haddock, pike or cod)
1 teaspoon salt	1 teaspoon salt
1 egg	1 egg
1½ tablespoons cornflour	2 tablespoons cornstarch
1 small head celery	1 small bunch celery
1 tablespoon light-coloured	1 tablespoon light-colored
soy sauce	soy sauce
1 teaspoon sesame oil	1 teaspoon sesame oil
½ teaspoon monosodium glutamate	½ teaspoon monosodium glutamate
(optional)	(optional)
25 g/1 oz cooked smoked ham	1 slice cooked smoked ham
vegetable oil for deep-frying	vegetable oil for deep-frying

Cut the fish first into thin slices, then cut again into matchstick-thin strips about 5 cm/2 inches long. Add the salt to the egg and beat well. Coat the fish with this mixture and then coat in cornflour. Wash the celery and cut into matchstick-thin strips. Plunge the celery for 30 seconds into boiling water. Then drain. Add the soy sauce, sesame oil and monosodium glutamate to the celery. Toss and mix well. Cut the ham into matchstick-thin strips.

Heat the oil to 180°C, 350°F, or until a day-old cube of bread turns golden in 1 minute. Using a frying basket, if possible, add the fish and spread the pieces out evenly with a pair of bamboo chopsticks. Deep-fry for 3 to 4 minutes, after which time the strips of fish will float to the surface. Remove and drain them. Place the celery mixture in a large heated serving dish. Arrange the fried fish on top. Mix gently. Use the ham to garnish the fish and celery.

NOTE   This 'salad' can be eaten with a chilli-soy dip (one part chilli sauce to six parts soy sauce).

Garnished steamed sole

Ch'ing Cheng Pien Yü

When cooking is done by plain steaming, the flavour depends — as it does in this dish — on marinating and garnishing. This recipe comes from the Ren Hua Lo Restaurant, Shanghai.

Serve for a family meal or party

METRIC/IMPERIAL	AMERICAN
2 sole, about 450 g/1 lb each	2 sole, about 1 lb each
2 teaspoons salt	2 teaspoons salt
3 tablespoons dry sherry	$\frac{1}{4}$ cup dry sherry
2 tablespoons chicken broth	3 tablespoons chicken broth
1 tablespoon castor sugar	1 tablespoon sugar
$\frac{1}{2}$ teaspoon monosodium glutamate (optional)	$\frac{1}{2}$ teaspoon monosodium glutamate (optional)
15 g/$\frac{1}{2}$ oz lard	1$\frac{1}{2}$ teaspoons lard
Garnish	*Garnish*
1 tablespoon diced pork fat	1 tablespoon diced fat back
2 slices cooked smoked ham	2 slices cooked smoked ham
25 g/1 oz bamboo shoots	$\frac{1}{4}$ cup bamboo shoots
2 spring onions	2 scallions
12 small dried Chinese mushrooms, soaked and drained	12 small dried Chinese mushrooms, soaked and drained
8 slices fresh root ginger	8 slices fresh ginger root

Clean the fish thoroughly and dry well. Rub on both sides with the salt and half the sherry. Cut three slashes on each side of the sole, halfway through the flesh. Place them on an oval ovenproof dish. Heat the broth. Add half the sugar, the monosodium glutamate, lard and remaining sherry and mix well. Sprinkle this mixture evenly over the fish.

Pile the diced pork fat and remaining sugar in the middle of each fish as a 'hub'. Cut the ham and bamboo shoots into 5-cm/2-inch thin strips, and cut the spring onions into 2·5-cm/1-inch segments. Use the ham and bamboo shoots to form two lines at right angles to each other, meeting at the 'hub'. Put the mushrooms, spring onions and ginger in the spaces. Cover and steam over high heat for 20 minutes. Wipe the edge of the dish with a cloth and bring directly to the table.

The squirrel fish

Sung Shu Yü

This dish is called squirrel *fish because as the sauce is poured over the fish, it 'chatters' like a squirrel.*

Serve for a family meal

METRIC/IMPERIAL	AMERICAN
1 (1·5-kg/3-lb) fish, (carp, bream or bass)	1 (3-lb) fish (carp or bass)
1 teaspoon salt	1 teaspoon salt
25 g/1 oz cornflour	$\frac{1}{4}$ cup cornstarch
1½ tablespoons castor sugar	2 tablespoons sugar
3 tablespoons vinegar	$\frac{1}{4}$ cup vinegar
1 tablespoon soy sauce	1 tablespoon soy sauce
5 tablespoons chicken broth	6 tablespoons chicken broth
25 g/1 oz bamboo shoots	$\frac{1}{4}$ cup bamboo shoots
6-8 dried Chinese mushrooms, soaked and drained	6-8 dried Chinese mushrooms, soaked and drained
vegetable oil for deep-frying	vegetable oil for deep-frying
1½ tablespoons chopped onion	2 tablespoons chopped onion
1½ teaspoons chopped fresh root ginger	1½ teaspoons chopped fresh ginger root
15 g/½ oz lard	1 tablespoon lard

Scale the fish and cut off the head. Slice open from head to tail and remove the bones. Clean thoroughly. Rub with salt, inside and out, and coat thoroughly with half the cornflour. Cut a dozen slashes with a knife on either side of the fish.

Mix the remaining cornflour, sugar, vinegar, soy sauce and chicken broth in a bowl. Cut the bamboo shoots into 1 × 2·5-cm/$\frac{1}{2}$ × 1-inch slices. Cut the mushrooms into strips.

Heat the oil to 180°C, 350°F, or until a day-old cube of bread turns golden in 1 minute. Place the fish in a wire basket. Lower it into very hot oil and deep-fry for 6 to 7 minutes. When the sizzling stops, reduce the heat. The fish will now have curled. Allow the fish to cook very slowly for 2 more minutes. Turn up the heat and quickly deep-fry the fish for a further 2 minutes. Drain and place on a heated oval dish.

Meanwhile, prepare the sauce by stir-frying the bamboo shoots, mushrooms, onion and ginger in the lard. After 2 minutes, pour in the cornflour mixture. Bring to the boil to thicken the sauce.

Bring the fish to the table immediately and pour the sauce over the fish at the table.

Red-cooked shad

Hung Shao Shih Yü

Shad is one of the rare fish which does not need descaling. This is a delicious fish dish from this area which specialises in fish recipes.

Serve for a banquet or family party

METRIC/IMPERIAL	AMERICAN
1 (1·75-2·25-kg/4-5-lb) shad, (see recipe)	1 (4-5-lb) shad, (see recipe)
2 tablespoons soy sauce	3 tablespoons soy sauce
25 g/1 oz bamboo shoots	$\frac{1}{4}$ cup bamboo shoots
1 tablespoon castor sugar	1 tablespoon sugar
2 tablespoons sherry	3 tablespoons sherry
1 teaspoon salt	1 teaspoon salt
1 tablespoon chopped fresh root ginger	1 tablespoon chopped fresh ginger root
1 tablespoon chopped onion	1 tablespoon chopped onion
25 g/1 oz dried Chinese mushrooms, soaked in 300 ml/ $\frac{1}{2}$ pint water	1 cup dried Chinese mushrooms, soaked in $1\frac{1}{4}$ cups water
40 g/1$\frac{1}{2}$ oz lard	3 tablespoons lard
15 g/$\frac{1}{2}$ oz pork fat	1 tablespoon fat back
1 tablespoon cornflour	1 tablespoon cornstarch

Remove the head and fins of the shad but not the scales, which are edible. Cut the fish in half lengthwise. Reserve half the fish for another dish. Clean and soak the remaining half in water for 1 hour.

Dry the fish and rub the scale-side with half the soy sauce. Slice the bamboo shoots. Mix the remaining soy sauce, bamboo shoots, sugar, sherry, salt, ginger, onion, mushrooms and mushroom water (obtained from soaking them) in a bowl.

Heat the lard in a frying pan. Cut the pork fat into cubes and fry for 2 minutes. Spread the cubes around the frying pan evenly and place the fish on top of them, scale-side down. Fry without stirring for 5 minutes. Turn the fish over and fry on the other side. After 1 minute, pour off the excess lard and add the mixed sauce. Lower the heat and simmer until cooked, about 15 minutes.

Lift the fish out on to a plate. Turn the heat to high then add to the fish liquid, the cornflour mixed with a little water. Bring to the boil and stir for 30 seconds until the sauce thickens. Then pour the sauce over the fish, and serve.

Prawn-topped pork

Fu-Yung Rou

This dish is said to have been derived from a recipe over a thousand years old, which was recently found and revived. It has become a popular feature on the menu of the Hongchow Restaurant in Chekiang.

Serve for a banquet or family meal

METRIC/IMPERIAL	AMERICAN
1 (450-g/1-lb) piece lean pork fillet	1 (1-lb) piece lean pork fillet
75 g/3 oz shredded suet	generous $\frac{1}{2}$ cup chopped suet
20 prawns, peeled	20 shrimp, shelled
vegetable oil for deep-frying	vegetable oil for deep-frying
2 tablespoons sesame oil	3 tablespoons sesame oil
1 tablespoon chopped red or green pepper	1 tablespoon chopped red or green pepper
1 tablespoon sherry	1 tablespoon sherry
$1\frac{1}{2}$ tablespoons soy sauce	2 tablespoons soy sauce
2 tablespoons wine-sediment paste (see page 171)	3 tablespoons wine-sediment paste (see page 171)
1 teaspoon monosodium glutamate (optional)	1 teaspoon monosodium glutamate (optional)

Slice the pork into twenty $5 \times 2 \cdot 5$-cm/2×1-inch thin slices. Divide the suet into 20 portions. Place the pork spread out to dry in an airy place for 4 hours.

Place a piece of suet on top of each piece of pork. Press the suet and pork firmly together by pounding with the end of a rolling pin or, traditionally, with the side of meat cleaver. Place a prawn on top of the suet and give it a further gentle pounding to flatten the prawn against the suet and pork.

Heat the vegetable oil to 180°C, 350°F, or until a day-old cube of bread turns golden in 1 minute. Deep-fry each piece of triple layer pork, suet and prawn for 1 minute. Drain and put aside.

Heat the sesame oil in a large frying pan and fry the chopped peppers until they turn black. Discard the peppers and remove the pan from the heat. Mix together the sherry, soy sauce, wine-sediment paste and monosodium glutamate. Arrange the pork pieces in the frying pan and sprinkle with the sherry mixture. Over a high heat, fry the prawn-topped pork on both sides, basting, for 1 minute. Serve immediately in a single layer on a well-heated plate.

Soochow melon chicken

Hsi Kua Chi

The whole small chicken is steamed inside a hollowed-out melon – the melon 'lid' is lifted off at the table to reveal the chicken inside.

Serve for a banquet

METRIC/IMPERIAL	AMERICAN
1 small (675-g/1½-lb) chicken	1 small 1½-lb chicken
1·15 litres/2 pints water	5 cups water
25 g/1 oz cooked smoked ham	¼ cup cooked smoked ham
40 g/1½ oz bamboo shoots	6 tablespoons bamboo shoots
8 dried Chinese mushrooms, soaked and drained	8 dried Chinese mushrooms, soaked and drained
4 slices fresh root ginger	4 slices fresh ginger root
1½ teaspoons salt	1½ teaspoons salt
2 tablespoons dry sherry	3 tablespoons dry sherry
1 large honeydew melon	1 large honeydew melon
1 teaspoon monosodium glutamate (optional)	1 teaspoon monosodium glutamate (optional)

Boil the chicken in the water for 2 minutes. Remove the chicken and rinse the bird in fresh water. Skim the broth. Thinly slice the ham and bamboo shoots, cut the mushrooms in strips and marinate in one-third of the broth, with the ginger, salt and sherry for about 30 minutes. Return the chicken to the remaining broth. Place in a steamer, cover and steam for 1 hour.

Cut a lid off the melon, set aside, and carefully scoop out the melon, leaving the wall at least 1 cm/½ inch thick. Reserve half the melon flesh for another dish.

Place the melon shell in a large bowl and fit the steamed chicken inside it, breast upwards. Arrange the ham, bamboo shoots and mushrooms on the chicken. Slip pieces of the melon flesh down the side around the chicken. Add the monosodium glutamate to the marinade and carefully pour this into the melon. Replace the lid of the melon and secure it with three cocktail sticks. Place the bowl in a steamer, cover and steam for 20 minutes. Remove the bowl from the steamer and bring it to the table. Lift off the melon lid and serve the chicken from the melon shell.

Salt pork with cabbage heart

(Illustrated on page 68)

Yen Jou T'sai Hsin

Vegetables grow in abundance in this part of China. For the sake of tenderness, often only the heart of cabbage is used. The outer leaves are fed to the pigs so that nothing is wasted. Salt beef could be substituted for pork in this dish.

Serve for a family meal

METRIC/IMPERIAL	AMERICAN
100 g/4 oz belly of pork or salt beef	$\frac{1}{4}$ lb salt pork or corned beef brisket
675 g/1$\frac{1}{2}$ lb cabbage or spring greens (see recipe)	1$\frac{1}{2}$ lb cabbage or lettuce (see recipe)
2 tablespoons vegetable oil	3 tablespoons vegetable oil
4 tablespoons chicken broth	$\frac{1}{3}$ cup chicken broth
1 teaspoon salt	1 teaspoon salt
$\frac{1}{2}$ teaspoon monosodium glutamate (optional)	$\frac{1}{2}$ teaspoon monosodium glutamate (optional)
1$\frac{1}{2}$ teaspoons lard	1$\frac{1}{2}$ teaspoons lard

Cut the meat into 1 × 3-cm/$\frac{1}{2}$ × 1$\frac{1}{2}$-inch paper-thin slices. Remove and discard the outer leaves and base of the cabbage, leaving only the tender inside leaves (or use spring greens). Cut these criss-cross into 5-cm/2-inch pieces.

Heat the oil in a pan over high heat. When very hot, add the cabbage and scramble-fry for 1$\frac{1}{2}$ minutes. Add the pork and broth. Sprinkle with the salt and monosodium glutamate. Stir-fry gently for 3 minutes. Add the lard and after a couple of stirs and tosses, transfer to a heated dish and serve.

Because of the very short period of cooking, the vegetable remains glistening green. Although a simple dish – usually an item of home cooking – it appeals to everyone.

Bean sprouts with shredded pork

(Illustrated on pages 106-107)

Tou Ya T'sai Ch'ao Jou Ssu

The dishes sold by the Municipal Caterers, of which this is a typical example, are seldom very elaborate. They are, therefore, easy to reproduce in the West.

Serve for a family meal

METRIC/IMPERIAL	AMERICAN
100 g/4 oz lean pork	$\frac{1}{4}$ lb lean pork
1 clove garlic	1 clove garlic
6 spring onions	6 scallions
2 tablespoons vegetable oil	3 tablespoons vegetable oil
1 tablespoon soy sauce	1 tablespoon soy sauce
2 teaspoons castor sugar	2 teaspoons sugar
1 tablespoon dry sherry	1 tablespoon dry sherry
675 g/1$\frac{1}{2}$ lb bean sprouts	1$\frac{1}{2}$ lb bean sprouts
1 teaspoon salt	1 teaspoon salt

Cut the pork across the grain into matchstick-thin strips. Crush the garlic and cut the spring onions into 8-cm/1$\frac{1}{2}$-inch segments. Heat the oil in a large frying pan. Add the meat and sauté over high heat for 30 seconds. Add the soy sauce, sugar and sherry. Stir-fry for 1 minute. Remove the meat and set aside to drain.

 Add the garlic and spring onions to the frying pan and stir-fry for 15 seconds. Add the bean sprouts and sprinkle with the salt. Stir-fry for 1 minute, keeping the pan over high heat. Replace the pork in the pan. After 1 minute of stir-frying, transfer to a heated dish and serve.

NOTE   Shredded meat dishes, when freshly and carefully served, rarely need any further decoration. The meat, sugar and soy sauce provide the necessary savouriness.

Right *Anchovy pork (see page 119).*
Overleaf *Shao Hsing soup (see page 84); Bean sprouts with shredded pork (see above); Riot of spring (see page 109).*

Riot of spring

(Illustrated on pages 106-107)

Tun T'sai Ho

*In this recipe, a vegetable is presented as an important dish on its own
merits. This often occurs in Chinese cooking.*

Serve for a banquet

METRIC/IMPERIAL	AMERICAN
2·25 kg/5 lb spring greens (compact, with firm hearts)	5 lb spring cabbages or lettuces (compact, with firm hearts)
1 breast of chicken	1 chicken breast
1 thin slice cooked smoked ham	1 thin slice cooked smoked ham
25 g/1 oz winter bamboo shoots	$\frac{1}{4}$ cup winter bamboo shoots
8 dried Chinese mushrooms, soaked and drained	8 dried Chinese mushrooms, soaked and drained
1 egg white	1 egg white
1 teaspoon cornflour	1 teaspoon cornstarch
450 ml/$\frac{3}{4}$ pint chicken broth	2 cups chicken broth
1 teaspoon salt	1 teaspoon salt
1 teaspoon monosodium glutamate (optional)	1 teaspoon monosodium glutamate (optional)
1 tablespoon chicken fat	1 tablespoon chicken fat
vegetable oil for deep-frying	vegetable oil for deep-frying
1 tablespoon dry sherry	1 tablespoon dry sherry

Cut off the stalks of the spring greens. Remove and discard the outer leaves
until each heart stands out like an upstanding, firm green bud. Cut the
breast of chicken into thin $1 \times 2 \cdot 5$-cm/$\frac{1}{2} \times 1$-inch slices. Slice the ham and
bamboo shoots in the same manner. Cut the mushrooms into 5-mm/$\frac{1}{4}$-inch
wide strips. Mix the egg white and cornflour in a bowl and dip the sliced
chicken in it.

Bring the chicken broth to the boil in a large pan. Add half the salt, half
the monosodium glutamate and half the chicken fat. Place the spring
greens in this mixture to boil for about 1 to $1\frac{1}{2}$ minutes.

Remove the spring greens and arrange the leaves to line the sides of a deep
ovenproof dish or casserole, reserving two or three hearts. Use these to
pack the middle, with three or four layers of tender leaves. Heat the oil to
180°C, 350°F, or until a day-old cube of bread turns golden in 1 minute and
deep-fry the slices of chicken for 45 seconds. Arrange them, together with
the ham, bamboo shoots and mushrooms in concentric rings on top of the
layers of green leaves. Pour in the broth and dot with the remaining chicken
fat. Sprinkle with the remaining salt, monosodium glutamate and the sherry.
Place in a steamer, cover and steam for 25 minutes. Serve in the casserole.

Left *Crispy ravioli soup with bamboo shoots (see page 122).*

Fukien

The province of Fukien, with a population of over 15 million and an area of 47,500 square miles, is situated approximately halfway along the coast between Shanghai and Canton. It has a mountainous, jagged coastline with many bays, gulfs, inlets and islands. This region is one of the few in South China which still produce timber despite centuries of using wood as fuel. Endless processions of timber rafts float down the Ming River past Foochow, the provincial capital.

Once, when I was preparing for my examinations, I was sitting with my brother on a hilltop overlooking the Ming, trying to memorize some passages, when an eagle flew down and hit both our heads with its wings — which shows that some of the remoter parts of the province must have been quite sparsely peopled, in spite of the general density of the population.

The climate here is semi-tropical; fruits of all kinds abound. There are numerous tangerine orchards and, beside the streams and tributaries, sugar (mostly the brown, unrefined variety) is produced locally from sugar cane. Many of the mountainsides and hilltops are covered with tea plantations, which produce some of the best-known brands of tea. Indeed, before the 1880's, Foochow was one of the greatest tea ports in the world. It was from the Ming River that the famous China clippers used to set sail for London or Liverpool. In the summer, under the scorching sun, the skins of the lychees shone bright red against the dark green leaves.

Fishing is an important industry here. At the height of the season, the fishing junks used to sail down the river to the open sea in fleets of several hundred. To watch them go was a memorable sight.

In its food and cuisine, Fukien is famous for the high quality of its soy sauce, for its special dough-skin made largely from meat, for its use of wine-sediment paste as a cooking ingredient, for its slow-fried dehydrated meat wool (see page 116), which is unparalleled for its excellence when eaten with soft rice or as a garnish, and for its emphasis on soup. A Cantonese friend of mine told me that he once had dinner with a Fukienose friend of his in Malaya and of the seven dishes on the table, four were soups!

Ming River

Foochow

Clams in chicken broth

(Illustrated on pages 126-127)

Chi T'ang Hai Pang

Clams are considered a delicacy in Fukien. They have white flesh and are generally served very lightly cooked. This recipe is one of the semi-soup dishes of which the people of Fukien are so fond. They are usually served in between the drier quick-fried or dry-fried dishes to provide a welcome break in variety and texture.

Serve for a banquet or family party

METRIC/IMPERIAL	AMERICAN
1·75 g/4 lb sea clams in shells or scallops	4 lb clams in shells or scallops
1 (450-675-g/1-1½-lb) chicken or chicken pieces	1 (1-1½-lb) chicken or chicken pieces
100 g/4 oz lean pork	¼ lb lean pork
1 slice fresh root ginger	1 slice fresh ginger root
900 ml/1½ pints water	3¾ cups water
2 tablespoons dry sherry	3 tablespoons dry sherry
1 tablespoon light-coloured soy sauce	1 tablespoon light-colored soy sauce
¾ teaspoon monosodium glutamate (optional)	¾ teaspoon monosodium glutamate (optional)

Cut away the body of the clams from their shells and clean the flesh thoroughly. Remove and discard the intestines. Cut the white flesh into halves and soak in fresh water. If using scallops, use only the white part.

Chop the chicken through the bone into four pieces and slice the pork into six pieces. Place the chicken and pork in boiling water to cover and boil for 1½ minutes. Drain and discard the water. Pack the chicken and pork, with the ginger, in a deep ovenproof casserole or pot and pour in the measured water. Cover and simmer, or steam in a steamer, for 2 hours.

When the chicken-pork broth is ready, place the clams in a bowl. Cover with boiling water and soak for 45 seconds. Drain and discard the water. Add the sherry to the clams and marinate for 1 minute. Discard the marinating liquid and place the clams in the bottom of a deep serving dish.

Remove the chicken and pork from the broth. The chicken and pork may be used in another recipe, if desired. Strain the broth and bring to the boil. Add the light-coloured soy sauce and monosodium glutamate. Pour the broth over the clams and serve immediately.

Swallow-skin ravioli soup

Jou Yen T'ang

The distinctive thing about this ravioli is that the dough is made largely of meat. Indeed, this type of meat-based dough seems unique to Fukien. When cooked, it feels firm and is transparent and tasty, but somehow not heavy. The soup is eaten more as a snack than as a meal. For some reason, this kind of dough is called 'swallow-skin', although born and bred in this region, I have never discovered why.

Serve for a family meal or party

METRIC/IMPERIAL	AMERICAN
Swallow-skin	*Swallow-skin*
675 g/1½ lb lean pork	1½ lb lean pork
100 g/4 oz cornflour	1 cup cornstarch
Filling	*Filling*
675 g/1½ lb lean and fat pork	1½ lb lean and fat pork
225 g/8 oz cooked peeled prawns	1 cup cooked shelled shrimp
225 g/8 oz water chestnuts	½ lb water chestnuts
225 g/8 oz bean curd (optional)	½ lb bean curd (optional)
100 g/4 oz spring onions	8-12 scallions
4 tablespoons soy sauce	⅓ cup soy sauce
2 litres/3½ pints superior broth	9 cups superior broth
(see page 170)	(see page 170)
1 teaspoon sesame oil	1 teaspoon sesame oil
1 teaspoon monosodium glutamate	1 teaspoon monosodium glutamate
(optional)	(optional)
freshly ground black pepper	freshly ground black pepper

Make the swallow-skin dough by finely mincing the lean pork twice. Place it in a mortar, add the cornflour and pound them together. Mix thoroughly. Place the mixture on a board and roll it out to a thin sheet. Cut into 5-cm/ 2-inch squares. To make the filling, finely mince the pork, prawns, water chestnuts, bean curd and half the spring onions. Blend with 3 tablespoons (U.S. ¼ cup) of the soy sauce.

To wrap the filling in the 'skin', place a teaspoon of filling into the middle of each square, held in the left palm. Fold the 'skin' over with the thumb and fingers and press together to seal.

Place the ravioli in a large pan of water. Bring to the boil and simmer for 5 minutes. Drain and discard the water. Place the *ravioli* in a large tureen. Heat the broth and pour into the tureen. Chop the remaining spring onions. Add the spring onions, the remaining soy sauce, the sesame oil, monosodium glutamate and pepper to taste. To serve, ladle the *ravioli* and soup into each individual bowl.

Silk-thread of bamboo shoots in chicken cream

Chi Yung Ching Chu Ssu

This is a dainty dish for those who do not have too large an appetite or for drinkers who only wish to nibble between sips. It may also be served as an introductory dish to a Chinese party meal.

Serve for a banquet

METRIC/IMPERIAL	AMERICAN
675 g/1½ lb bamboo shoots	1½ lb bamboo shoots
1 breast of chicken	1 chicken breast
40 g/1½ oz pork fat	3 tablespoons fat back
6 eggs	6 eggs
1 tablespoon cornflour	1 tablespoon cornstarch
1 teaspoon salt	1 teaspoon salt
½ teaspoon monosodium glutamate (optional)	½ teaspoon monosodium glutamate (optional)
2-3 sprigs parsley	2-3 sprigs parsley
300 ml/½ pint chicken broth	1¼ cups chicken broth
25 g/1 oz lard	2 tablespoons lard
1 tablespoon chopped cooked ham	1 tablespoon chopped cooked ham

Cut the bamboo shoots first into 3-5-cm/1½-2-inch lengths. Then, with a very sharp knife, cut again into the thinnest possible slices. Finally, cut the slices into very fine strips (about half the thickness of matchsticks). Mince the chicken flesh and pork fat twice. Beat the eggs in a bowl. Add the cornflour, salt and monosodium glutamate and beat to an even consistency. Wash the parsley, separate into small sprigs and discard the coarser stems. Place the bamboo shoots in a saucepan. Add the chicken broth and simmer for 25 to 30 minutes or until practically dry. Meanwhile, mix the chicken and pork fat with the egg mixture. Heat the lard in a frying pan. Add the bamboo shoots and stir-fry for 2 minutes. Add the chicken mixture and stir-fry gently for 2½ minutes. Transfer to a heated serving plate and garnish with the sprigs of parsley and the chopped ham.

The crunchiness of the bamboo shoots adds a new dimension to the scrambled eggs, which are made savoury by the monosodium glutamate and chicken, smooth by the lard and colourful by the ham and parsley.

Amoy pork escalope

(Illustrated on pages 126-127)

Tsa Li Jou

There is a well-known Fukien banquet called the 'Whole Pig Feast', in which a pig is slaughtered specially for the feast and made into 108 dishes. This is one of the typical dishes.

Serve for a family meal or party

METRIC/IMPERIAL	AMERICAN
1 (900-g/2-lb) piece belly of pork (with good proportion of lean meat to fat)	1 (2-lb) piece salt pork (with good proportion of lean meat to fat)
2 tablespoons soy sauce	3 tablespoons soy sauce
2 tablespoons dry sherry	3 tablespoons dry sherry
2 bay leaves	2 bay leaves
1 tablespoon brown rock sugar (see page 163)	1 tablespoon brown rock sugar (see page 163)
100 g/4 oz carrots	$\frac{1}{4}$ lb carrots
6 radishes	6 radishes
2 teaspoons salt	2 teaspoons salt
1 tablespoon castor sugar	1 tablespoon sugar
1 tablespoon vinegar	1 tablespoon vinegar
1 teaspoon sesame oil	1 teaspoon sesame oil
2 duck eggs (or 2 large eggs)	2 duck eggs (or 2 large eggs)
65 g/2$\frac{1}{2}$ oz breadcrumbs	1 cup bread crumbs
vegetable oil for deep-frying	vegetable oil for deep-frying

Boil the pork in water to cover for 5 minutes. Drain and cut into slices containing both lean meat and fat. Place the pork in an ovenproof bowl and add the soy sauce, sherry, bay leaves and rock sugar. Marinate for 30 minutes. Place the bowl of marinated pork in a steamer. Cover and steam for 1 hour. Remove and cool, then refrigerate until cold.

Meanwhile, shred the carrots and radishes into a colander, rub the salt into them and let stand for 10 minutes. Rinse them under cold water, drain and dry. Put the shredded carrots and radishes in a bowl and add the sugar, vinegar and sesame oil.

When the pork is quite cold and solid, break the eggs into a bowl, beat them lightly and dip each piece of pork in the egg. Roll the pieces of pork in the breadcrumbs until completely covered. Heat the vegetable oil to 180°C, 350°F, or until a day-old cube of bread turns golden in 1 minute, and deep-fry the pork (a few pieces at a time) for 3 minutes or until golden. Cut each slice of pork into three pieces.

Arrange the pieces of breadcrumbed pork around a mound of shredded radishes and carrots in the middle of the serving plate. The pork is crispy, very tender and extremely tasty.

Fukien meat 'wool'

Fukien Jou Sung

The meat 'wool' is a rich brownish-red in colour. It is usually served in small plates or saucers. It is not used at banquets, but it may be served with any combination of dishes in home cooking. For the initiated, it is one of the culinary wonders of the world.

Serve for a family meal

METRIC/IMPERIAL	AMERICAN
1 (1·5-kg/3-lb) boned lean leg of pork	1 (3-lb) boned lean leg of pork
1·15 litres/2 pints water	5 cups water
3 tablespoons soy sauce	$\frac{1}{4}$ cup soy sauce
2 teaspoons salt	2 teaspoons salt
2 tablespoons castor sugar	3 tablespoons sugar
5 tablespoons dry sherry	6 tablespoons dry sherry
1 tablespoon tomato purée	1 tablespoon tomato paste
75 g/3 oz lard	6 tablespoons lard

Clean and carefully remove every piece of gristle and fat from the pork. Cut the meat across the grain into 3-cm/$1\frac{1}{2}$-inch thick pieces. Slice it with the grain into $0.5 \times 1 \times 3$-cm/$\frac{1}{4} \times \frac{1}{2} \times 1\frac{1}{2}$-inch strips. Put the pork pieces in a saucepan. Add the water, soy sauce, salt, sugar, sherry and tomato purée. Bring to the boil. Then lower the heat to a minimum. Place an asbestos mat under the saucepan and simmer for $3\frac{1}{2}$ hours. By this time, there should not be more than 300 ml/$\frac{1}{2}$ pint (U.S. $1\frac{1}{4}$ cups) of liquid left in the pan.

Pour the pork and the liquid into a large frying pan. Place the pan over very low heat, stir and turn the pork with a wooden spoon, gently pulling apart the strips of meat to separate the fibres. This should continue for up to 1 hour or until the meat has completely dried. To ensure that the meat does not burn, place an asbestos mat under the pan during the latter stage of this dry-frying. When the meat has completely dried, add 25 g/1 oz (U.S. 2 tablespoons) of the lard and continue to stir-fry (over the very lowest heat) for 15 minutes. Thereafter, add 15 g/$\frac{1}{2}$ oz (U.S. 1 tablespoon) of the lard every 15 minutes. After about an hour of frying and intermittent stirring (in the later stages the speed of the stirring should be increased to prevent any burning), the pork will have turned into the anticipated meat 'wool'. Keep in a jar or bottle and use when required.

Deep-fried fish
in red wine-sediment paste

Cha Tsao Yü Kuai

This is an aromatic and wine-flavoured dish, suitable for eating with rice or just to nibble with a drink. The Restaurant of the Gallant Heart, from which this recipe comes, is situated beside the Hung Shan Bridge. As you drink and nibble, you can watch the boats shooting down the rapids.

Serve for a family meal or party

METRIC/IMPERIAL	AMERICAN
1 (900-g/2-lb) piece fresh fish	1 (2-lb) piece fresh fish
(haddock, cod, halibut or bass)	(haddock, cod, halibut or bass)
1 teaspoon salt	1 teaspoon salt
3 tablespoons dry sherry	$\frac{1}{4}$ cup dry sherry
3 tablespoons red wine-sediment	$\frac{1}{4}$ cup red wine-sediment
paste (see page 171)	paste (see page 171)
2 spring onions	2 scallions
vegetable oil for deep-frying	vegetable oil for deep-frying
1 tablespoon lard	1 tablespoon lard
1 tablespoon chopped fresh	1 tablespoon chopped fresh
root ginger	ginger root
1 tablespoon chopped onion	1 tablespoon chopped onion
1 teaspoon castor sugar	1 teaspoon sugar
1 teaspoon soy sauce	1 teaspoon soy sauce
2 tablespoons chicken or superior	3 tablespoons chicken or superior
broth (see page 170)	broth (see page 170)
$\frac{1}{2}$ teaspoon monosodium glutamate	$\frac{1}{2}$ teaspoon monosodium glutamate
(optional)	(optional)

Cut the fish into $2 \cdot 5 \times 3 \times 5$-cm/$1 \times 1\frac{1}{2} \times 2$-inch thick pieces. Rub with the salt and marinate in a mixture of half the sherry and half the red wine-sediment paste for 1 hour. Cut the spring onions into 3-cm/$1\frac{1}{2}$-inch segments.

Heat the vegetable oil to 180°C, 350°F, or until a day-old cube of bread turns golden in 1 minute and deep-fry the fish in it for 3 to 4 minutes. Drain on absorbent kitchen paper for 1 minute. Then arrange the red chunks of fish on a large flat plate.

Heat the lard in a small frying pan. Add the ginger and onion and sauté over high heat for 1 minute. Add the remaining sherry, remaining wine-sediment paste, the sugar, soy sauce, chicken or superior broth and monosodium glutamate. Continue to stir-fry for 30 seconds. Pour the sauce over the fish, garnish with the spring onions and serve.

Pine-flower meat soufflé omelette

Sung Hua Jou

This is, in fact, a famous Foochow dish. Its attractiveness lies in its colour and in the appealing aroma of sherry applied at the last moment. If brandy were used, it could probably be flamed. But brandy, alas, is not a product of the region!

Serve for a family meal

METRIC/IMPERIAL	AMERICAN
6 eggs	6 eggs
25 g/1 oz plain flour	$\frac{1}{4}$ cup all-purpose flour
1 teaspoon salt	1 teaspoon salt
1 teaspoon monosodium glutamate (optional)	1 teaspoon monosodium glutamate (optional)
100 g/4 oz lean pork	$\frac{1}{4}$ lb lean pork
2 spring onions	2 scallions
25 g/1 oz dried Chinese mushrooms, soaked and drained	1 cup dried Chinese mushrooms, soaked and drained
25 g/1 oz bamboo shoots	$\frac{1}{4}$ cup bamboo shoots
1 teaspoon castor sugar	1 teaspoon sugar
1 tablespoon soy sauce	1 tablespoon soy sauce
$\frac{1}{4}$ teaspoon five-spice powder (optional, see page 160)	$\frac{1}{4}$ teaspoon five-spice powder (optional, see page 160)
75 g/3 oz lard	6 tablespoons lard
2 tablespoons chopped parsley	3 tablespoons chopped parsley
1 tablespoon dry sherry	1 tablespoon dry sherry

Separate the egg whites from the yolks. Beat the whites for 2 minutes or until nearly stiff. Fold in the yolks, flour, salt and monosodium glutamate. Finely chop the pork and spring onions. Slice the mushrooms and bamboo shoots into matchstick-thin strips. Place the pork, spring onions, mushrooms, bamboo shoots, sugar, soy sauce and five-spice powder in a bowl. Mix well.

Heat 15 g/$\frac{1}{2}$ oz (U.S. 1 tablespoon) of the lard in a small pan. Add the pork mixture and stir-fry for 3 minutes. Remove from the heat and set aside. Place half the remaining lard in a large frying pan over very low heat. When the lard has melted, add half the egg mixture, which will spread into a 15-cm/6-inch diameter circle. When the egg has somewhat set, gently put the cooked pork mixture into the centre.

After 1 minute of cooking over low heat, pour the remainder of the egg mixture over the filling. Heat the remaining lard in a small saucepan until very hot and pour it over the soft egg mixture. Sprinkle the parsley over the omelette then pour over the sherry. Cook for 30 seconds without stirring. Then lift one side of the omelette to drain away the lard. Use a large spatula to lift the omelette on to a heated serving plate and serve immediately.

Anchovy pork

(Illustrated on page 105)

Yen Yü Tun Chu Jou

The flavour of fresh meat or vegetables is often enhanced by cooking with dried or pickled food. In this recipe, fresh pork is cooked with salted fish, giving it a unique flavour and a saltiness particularly attractive to rice-eaters.

Serve for a family meal

METRIC/IMPERIAL	AMERICAN
1 (900-g/2-lb) piece belly of pork	1 (2-lb) piece salt pork
2 tablespoons chopped onion	3 tablespoons chopped onion
4 slices fresh root ginger	4 slices fresh ginger root
1 teaspoon salt	1 teaspoon salt
300 ml/$\frac{1}{2}$ pint water	$1\frac{1}{4}$ cups water
6-12 canned or dried anchovy fillets, according to taste	6-12 canned or dried anchovy fillets, according to taste

Plunge the pork into boiling water to cover and simmer for 10 minutes. Drain and slice the pork across the meat, fat and skin, so that each piece measures about $1 \times 2.5 \times 5$ cm/$\frac{1}{2} \times 1 \times 2$ inches and has skin attached. Arrange the pork, skin-side down, in a casserole. Place the onion, ginger and salt in a small saucepan, add the $\frac{1}{2}$ pint water, bring to the boil and simmer for 5 minutes. Remove from the heat and pour the contents of the pan over the pork. Arrange the anchovy fillets on top of the pork.

Place the casserole in a large saucepan filled with 2.5-3 cm/1-$1\frac{1}{2}$ inches water. It is essential that the water should not reach more than halfway up the side of the casserole. Bring the water to the boil, cover and simmer over a very low heat for $1\frac{1}{2}$ hours (adding water to the saucepan when necessary). Alternatively, the pork may be steamed for $1\frac{1}{4}$ hours.

After this fairly long cooking period, the taste and saltiness of the anchovy fillets will have penetrated the pork, including the skin, which should be almost jelly-like in tenderness.

Cantonese Cooking

Cantonese cooking, which is that of the province of Kwangtung, of which Canton is the capital, has the largest collection of regional dishes in the whole of China. Apart from French cuisine, Cantonese cooking alone probably possesses a larger repertoire of dishes than any other area. The fact that it is only one of a dozen regional schools of China is witness to the enormous size and range of Chinese cooking.

For those who are used to the comparatively chunkier, less fussy and more piquant cooking of Peking and the North, Cantonese cooking seems to be characterised by its infinite elaboration, it use of unclassical materials and its addiction to a wide range of fruit skins, herbs, sauces and seafood. But to those who hold the opinion that the finest cooking, like the finest fashion, must, to a degree, reflect human indulgence and degeneration, Cantonese cooking must be classified as one of the most refined, self-indulgent and degenerate in the whole of China!

To a large extent, food and cuisine must necessarily be the product of the geography of the region. Geographically, Kwangtung is the Louisiana of China, and Canton, her New Orleans, although as a city, Canton is more important industrially than New Orleans, and as a province, Kwangtung is much larger and more heavily populated than Louisiana. It has a population of over 40 million and a coastline which zigzags for nearly a thousand miles. Its principal cities and towns are situated along the Pearl River and its tributaries—the West River and the smaller East River.

It was from here that the main bulk of Chinese emigrants went abroad to develop and enrich themselves in the South Seas. In the 19th century, several tens of thousands of them crossed the Pacific to San Francisco, where they founded the famous Chinatown, helped to build the Union Pacific railway, evolved Chopsuey and introduced it to the United States.

The climate of Kwangtung is temperate, verging on the semi-tropical, and fruit grows in abundance. Add to this its long coastline and the former wealth and leisure of its bourgeoisie, and there is little wonder that the cooking in this region has a large preoccupation with seafood, fruit and tea-house food.

In making a selection of recipes derived from actual restaurants and eating houses situated in the area, I have deliberately omitted those recipes which are obviously unacceptable (such as those using snakes, wild cats and puppies), or those recipes where the ingredients and materials are difficult to find.

Kwangtung

Crispy ravioli soup with bamboo shoots

(Illustrated on page 108)

Mu Erh Hun Tun T'ang

Very thin-skinned ravioli are used in this soup as croûtons are used in western soups. Wood-ears are used for texture and variation rather than taste. Button mushrooms may be substituted.

Serve for a banquet or family meal

METRIC/IMPERIAL	AMERICAN
Hun Tun skin	*Hun Tun skin*
175 g/6 oz plain flour	1½ cups all-purpose flour
salt	salt
4 tablespoons water	⅓ cup water
½ teaspoon lard	½ teaspoon lard
Filling	*Filling*
½ small onion	½ small onion
2 water chestnuts	2 water chestnuts
50 g/2 oz pork	¼ cup pork
1 teaspoon sesame oil	1 teaspoon sesame oil
Soup	*Soup*
15 g/½ oz wood-ears, soaked for 1 hour	½ cup wood-ears, soaked for 1 hour
40 g/1½ oz heart of spring greens	½ cup spring lettuce or cabbage heart
2 tablespoons chopped leeks	3 tablespoons chopped leeks
2 slices fresh root ginger	2 slices fresh ginger root
300 ml/½ pint water	1¼ cups water
900 ml/1½ pints superior broth (see page 170)	3¾ cups superior broth (see page 170)
1½ tablespoons soy sauce	2 tablespoons soy sauce
40 g/1½ oz bamboo shoots	6 tablespoons bamboo shoots
½ teaspoon sesame oil	½ teaspoon sesame oil
1 teaspoon monosodium glutamate (optional)	1 teaspoon monosodium glutamate (optional)
salt and freshly ground black pepper	salt and freshly ground black pepper
vegetable oil for deep-frying	vegetable oil for deep-frying

Prepare the *Hun Tun* skin as for *Chinese swallow-skin ravioli* (see page 137). After kneading, cut into 24 portions and roll each portion into a very thin dough.

For the filling, chop the onion and water chestnuts and finely mince the pork. Heat the sesame oil in a small pan and sauté the onion, water chestnuts and pork for 2 minutes. Remove from the heat and cool. Divide into 24 portions. Wrap a portion of filling in each dough skin.

For the soup, boil the wood-ears together with the spring greens in water to cover for 5 minutes. Discard the water. Boil the leeks and ginger in the 300 ml/½ pint (U.S. 1¼ cups) water for 10 minutes. Add the wood-ears, spring greens, one third of the superior broth, the soy sauce and bamboo shoots. Simmer for 10 minutes.

Pour this soup into a large ovenproof tureen. Add the sesame oil, remaining superior broth, the monosodium glutamate and season to taste. Steam for 15 minutes (see page 172). Heat the oil to 180°C, 350°F, or until a day-old cube of bread turns golden in 1 minute, and deep-fry the *ravioli* for 4 minutes, or until golden.

Place the fried *ravioli* at the bottom of a large, heated tureen and pour over the soup. Bring to the dinner table quickly, while the crackling *ravioli* is 'singing' in the tureen, and serve immediately.

Cream of Chinese cabbage soup

Nai Yu Pai T'sai T'ang

This is a pleasant soup for a home meal. The use of milk is a sign of western influence, which is occasionally noticeable in Cantonese cooking.

Serve for a family meal

METRIC/IMPERIAL	AMERICAN
450 g/1 lb Chinese celery cabbage	1 lb Chinese celery cabbage
600 ml/1 pint superior broth (see page 170)	2½ cups superior broth (see page 170)
1 teaspoon salt	1 teaspoon salt
freshly ground black pepper	freshly ground black pepper
300 ml/½ pint milk	1¼ cups milk
15 g/½ oz lard	1 tablespoon lard
1 teaspoon monosodium glutamate (optional)	1 teaspoon monosodium glutamate (optional)
1 tablespoon cornflour	1 tablespoon cornstarch
2 tablespoons water	3 tablespoons water

Cut the cabbage into 1 × 2·5-cm/½ × 1-inch pieces. Wash thoroughly. Heat the broth. Add the cabbage and simmer for 15 minutes. Add the salt, pepper to taste, milk, lard and monosodium glutamate. Bring to the boil. Add the cornflour blended with the water and simmer for a further 5 minutes. Serve in a heated tureen. This is a very simple, but delicious soup for serving with rice.

Chicken velvet and corn soup

Chi Yung Shu Mi

*This soup is often served in Cantonese homes. It is easy to make and quick
to serve, and is particularly acceptable to the western palate as sweet corn
is a familiar and favourite food.*

Serve for a family meal

METRIC/IMPERIAL	AMERICAN
1 breast of chicken	1 chicken breast
2 egg whites	2 egg whites
900 ml/1½ pints chicken broth (see note)	3¾ cups chicken broth (see note)
1 (198-g/7-oz) can sweetcorn kernels	1 (7-oz) can sweetcorn kernels
1 tablespoon cornflour	1 tablespoon cornstarch
3 tablespoons water	¼ cup water
2 tablespoons fresh green peas	3 tablespoons fresh green peas
1 teaspoon salt	1 teaspoon salt
½ teaspoon monosodium glutamate (optional)	½ teaspoon monosodium glutamate (optional)
25 g/1 oz cooked smoked ham	1 thin slice cooked smoked ham

Finely mince the chicken flesh and mix thoroughly in a bowl with the egg
whites. Bring the chicken broth to the boil in a pan. Add the sweet corn
and then stir in the cornflour mixed with the water. When the contents
reboil, stir in the chicken mixture. Stirring gently, add the peas, salt and
monosodium glutamate. Simmer for 5-6 minutes over low heat. Chop the
ham finely. Pour the soup into a heated tureen or large soup dish and
garnish with the chopped ham before serving.

NOTE   The chicken broth used in this recipe may either be purchased in
liquid form or made from 2 chicken stock cubes.

Right Chinese ravioli with prawn-pork filling (see page 137).
Overleaf *Amoy pork escalope (see page 115); Clams in chicken broth (see page 112).*
Shown on page 128 *Sweet and sour pork (see page 129).*

Sweet and sour pork

(Illustrated opposite)

Ku Lao Jou

This dish requires no introduction since it is probably the most famous Chinese dish in the West. It is important to keep the pork crispy and distinctively tasty although immersed in a very pronounced sweet and sour sauce. The latter, when well made, is translucent and has a fruity, refreshing taste.

Serve for a family meal or party

METRIC/IMPERIAL	AMERICAN
1 (225-g/8-oz) piece belly of pork	1 ($\frac{1}{2}$-lb) piece salt pork
1 teaspoon salt	1 teaspoon salt
1 tablespoon dry sherry	1 tablespoon dry sherry
1 egg	1 egg
1 tablespoon cornflour	1 tablespoon cornstarch
1 sweet green or red pepper	1 sweet green or red pepper
1 leek	1 leek
$\frac{1}{2}$ small onion	$\frac{1}{2}$ small onion
50 g/2 oz bamboo shoots	$\frac{1}{2}$ cup bamboo shoots
5 tablespoons vegetable oil	6 tablespoons vegetable oil
Sweet and Sour sauce	*Sweet and Sour sauce*
50 g/2 oz brown sugar	$\frac{1}{2}$ cup brown sugar
2 tablespoons white vinegar	3 tablespoons white vinegar
1 tablespoon tangerine or orange juice	1 tablespoon tangerine or orange juice
1 tablespoon tomato purée	1 tablespoon tomato paste
1 tablespoon soy sauce	1 tablespoon soy sauce
1 tablespoon cornflour	1 tablespoon cornstarch

Cut away the skin from the pork. Dice the flesh into 1-cm/$\frac{1}{2}$-inch cubes. Add the salt and sherry and marinate for 30 minutes. Make a batter with the egg mixed with the cornflour. Trim and deseed the pepper and cut into thin strips. Cut the leek into 1-cm/$\frac{1}{2}$-inch sections. Chop the onion and the bamboo shoots into 0·5 × 1 × 1-cm/$\frac{1}{4}$ × $\frac{1}{2}$ × $\frac{1}{2}$-inch slices.

For the sauce, mix together the brown sugar, vinegar, tangerine or orange juice, tomato purée and soy sauce. Heat the mixture in a small pan until the sugar dissolves completely. Remove the pan from the heat.

Coat the pork in the batter. Heat the oil in a frying pan. Pour in the pork and stir-fry gently over high heat for 2$\frac{1}{2}$ minutes. Add the bamboo shoots and continue to stir-fry for 30 seconds. Remove the pork and bamboo shoots and set aside. Pour off the excess oil.

Replace the frying pan over the heat and add the pepper, leek and onion. Stir-fry for 1 minute. Add the cornflour to the sweet and sour sauce, blend well and pour it into the pan. Stir gently until the contents reboil. Add the partially-cooked pork and bamboo shoots. After a few quick stirs and scrambles, transfer to a heated serving plate and serve.

Spare ribs braised in fruit juice

Kuo Chih Kuo Pai Ku

Spare ribs are very popular in Chinese restaurants in the West. This recipe, with its bold use of fruit juices, is a most unusual one.

Serve for a family meal or party

METRIC/IMPERIAL	AMERICAN
900 g/2 lb meaty pork spare ribs	2 lb meaty pork spareribs
2 tablespoons finely chopped leeks	3 tablespoons finely chopped leeks
1 teaspoon salt	1 teaspoon salt
2 teaspoons castor sugar	2 teaspoons sugar
1½ tablespoons light-coloured soy sauce	2 tablespoons light-colored soy sauce
½ teaspoon monosodium glutamate (optional)	½ teaspoon monosodium glutamate (optional)
1 tablespoon cornflour	1 tablespoon cornstarch
3 tablespoons vegetable oil	¼ cup vegetable oil
2 tablespoons chopped onion	3 tablespoons chopped onion
1 tablespoon apple juice	1 tablespoon apple juice
1 tablespoon orange juice	1 tablespoon orange juice
1 tablespoon tomato purée	1 tablespoon tomato paste
5 tablespoons secondary broth (see page 163)	6 tablespoons secondary broth (see page 163)
2 tablespoons dry sherry	3 tablespoons dry sherry

Separate each rib and chop across the bone into 2·5-cm/1-inch lengths or leave whole. Combine the leeks with the salt, sugar, soy sauce and monosodium glutamate in a bowl. Add the spare ribs and marinate for 30 minutes. Dust with cornflour and mix well.

Heat the oil in a frying pan, add the ribs and stir-fry gently for 25 minutes or until golden. Drain off the excess oil and set the ribs aside.

Sauté the onion for 1 minute in the oil remaining in the pan. Add the spare ribs. Pour in the apple juice, orange juice, tomato purée, broth and sherry. Stir-fry for 1 minute. Cover the pan and cook for 5-6 minutes, or until the liquid has largely evaporated. Serve on a heated dish.

NOTE Although simple in preparation, the dish has an interesting flavour. At the Chinese dinner table, an extra plate is provided for every diner in which to place the bones.

Sliced steak in oyster sauce

Hao Yu Niu Jou

This mingling of sea-taste with meat is typically Cantonese. This is one of the favourite and best-known dishes as prepared at the Ya Gai Restaurant, Canton. This is an excellent party dish since it is comparatively easy to prepare. Ideally, it should be eaten immediately.

Serve for a banquet or family meal

METRIC/IMPERIAL	AMERICAN
1 (225-g/8-oz) rump or fillet steak	1 ($\frac{1}{2}$-lb) beef tenderloin
2 tablespoons dry sherry	3 tablespoons dry sherry
1 tablespoon soy sauce	1 tablespoon soy sauce
1 tablespoon cornflour	1 tablespoon cornstarch
1 tablespoon water	1 tablespoon water
5 tablespoons vegetable oil	6 tablespoons vegetable oil
1$\frac{1}{2}$ tablespoons oyster sauce	2 tablespoons oyster sauce
(see page 161)	(see page 161)
3 tablespoons superior broth	$\frac{1}{4}$ cup superior broth
(see page 170)	(see page 170)
4-6 spring onions	4-6 scallions
3 slices fresh root ginger	3 slices fresh ginger root

Cut the meat across the grain into thin 2·5 × 3-cm/1 × 1$\frac{1}{2}$-inch slices. Place in a bowl together with half the sherry, the soy sauce and half the cornflour blended with the water. Mix thoroughly. Add 1 tablespoon of the vegetable oil and work it into the meat with your fingers.

In another bowl, mix together the remaining cornflour, the oyster sauce and broth. Cut the spring onions into 2·5-cm/1-inch segments, using the white part only. Heat the remaining vegetable oil in a frying pan over high heat. When very hot, add the beef and stir-fry for 30 seconds. Remove the beef and discard the excess oil. Replace the pan over the heat and sauté the spring onions and ginger for 20 seconds.

Replace the beef in the pan and pour in the remaining sherry. Spread the beef evenly in the pan. Quickly pour in the oyster sauce mixture. Stir-scramble for about 8-10 seconds over high heat and transfer to a heated plate before serving.

Clear-steamed fish

Ching Chen Yü

The Chinese concept of a good fish dish is like the western concept of a roast – something which may be carved or cut up at the table.

Serve for a family meal or party

METRIC/IMPERIAL	AMERICAN
1 (900-g-1·5-kg/2-3-lb) fish (grey mullet, bass, bream or carp)	1 (2-3-lb) fish (grey mullet, bass or carp)
1½ teaspoons salt	1½ teaspoons salt
2 teaspoons sesame oil	2 teaspoons sesame oil
1 teaspoon monosodium glutamate (optional)	1 teaspoon monosodium glutamate (optional)
25 g/1 oz lean pork	1 slice lean pork
2 teaspoons chopped fresh root ginger	2 teaspoons chopped fresh ginger root
2 tablespoons soy sauce	3 tablespoons soy sauce
2 teaspoons castor sugar	2 teaspoons sugar
4 spring onion tops	4 scallion stems
15 g/½ oz lard	1 tablespoon lard
4-6 dried Chinese mushrooms, soaked and drained	4-6 dried Chinese mushrooms, soaked and drained
2 tablespoons superior broth (see page 170)	¼ cup superior broth (see page 170)
2 tablespoons dry sherry	3 tablespoons dry sherry
1 teaspoon cornflour	1 teaspoon cornstarch
salt and freshly ground black pepper	salt and freshly ground black pepper

Clean the fish. Rub the inside with a mixture of the salt, sesame oil and half the monosodium glutamate. Cut the pork into matchstick-thin strips. Add the ginger, half the soy sauce and sugar to the pork. Chop two of the spring onion tops, add to the mixture and set aside. Chop each of the remaining spring onion tops into four to six segments. Put these in a large oval oven-proof dish. Place the fish on top and put the dish in a steamer. Cover and steam (20 minutes for a 900-g/2-lb fish, 30 minutes for a 1·4-kg/3-lb fish and upward).

Heat the lard in a frying pan. Slice the mushrooms and sauté for 5 seconds. Add the pork mixture and stir-fry over high heat. Blend the remaining soy sauce and monosodium glutamate, broth, sherry and cornflour. Add the mixture to the pan. Season to taste. Stir-fry and then pour the mixture over the fish and serve immediately.

Prawn-pork stuffed Pacific prawns

Ch'ien Niang Ming Hsia

*The Pacific prawns are stuffed to make them fatter and more succulent.
They may be eaten as they are, or with dips to give extra flavour.*

Serve for a banquet

METRIC/IMPERIAL	AMERICAN
8 large fresh Pacific prawns	8 large raw shrimp
2 tablespoons white wine	3 tablespoons white wine
1 teaspoon salt	1 teaspoon salt
$\frac{1}{2}$ teaspoon monosodium glutamate (optional)	$\frac{1}{2}$ teaspoon monosodium glutamate (optional)
100 g/4 oz cooked, peeled prawns (see recipe)	$\frac{1}{4}$ lb cooked, shelled shrimp (see recipe)
50 g/2 oz pork fat	$\frac{1}{4}$ cup fat back
2 eggs	2 eggs
4-5 tablespoons breadcrumbs	about $\frac{1}{3}$ cup bread crumbs
4 tablespoons vegetable oil	$\frac{1}{3}$ cup vegetable oil
watercress to garnish	watercress to garnish

Clean the Pacific prawns thoroughly and remove the shells. Marinate in the wine, salt and monosodium glutamate for 2 hours in the refrigerator.

To prepare a prawn-pork paste, mince the cooked prawns and the pork fat. Lightly beat the eggs and add 2-3 tablespoons (U.S. 3-4 tablespoons) of the beaten egg to the prawn-pork mixture, then mix together and knead until quite springy. Place in the refrigerator for 2 hours. Crabmeat may be used instead of prawns.

When the prawns and the prawn-pork paste are ready, stuff the belly of each prawn with 1 teaspoon of the paste. Dip each stuffed prawn in the remaining beaten egg and coat heavily with breadcrumbs.

Heat the vegetable oil in a large frying pan for 2 minutes. Remove from the heat and spread the prawns out in the pan. Return the pan to the heat and sauté gently for $2\frac{1}{2}$ minutes, turning the prawns over once or twice. Add more oil, if necessary. Sauté (without stirring) for another $2\frac{1}{2}$ minutes, cooking the prawns equally on all sides.

The prawns should be arranged in the middle of a heated dish surrounded by sprigs of watercress. Dips which would enhance the flavour of the prawns and which should be placed on the table are salt and pepper mix, orange juice, Plum sauce and soy sauce with a dash of chilli sauce.

Paper-wrapped chicken

(Illustrated on pages 146–147)

Chih Pao Chi

*This dish is easy to make. It should be popular if only for its novelty.
Chicken prepared like this is, in fact, superbly tasty. All the oil is kept out
by the greaseproof paper.*

Serve for a banquet

METRIC/IMPERIAL	AMERICAN
1 (900-g/2-lb) chicken or chicken pieces	1 (2-lb) chicken or chicken pieces
2 tablespoons soy sauce	3 tablespoons soy sauce
2 tablespoons dry sherry	3 tablespoons dry sherry
1 tablespoon castor sugar	1 tablespoon sugar
3 slices fresh root ginger	3 slices fresh ginger root
$\frac{1}{2}$ teaspoon monosodium glutamate (optional)	$\frac{1}{2}$ teaspoon monosodium glutamate (optional)
1 large sheet greaseproof paper	1 large sheet parchment paper
vegetable oil for deep-frying	vegetable oil for deep-frying
green vegetables to garnish	green vegetables to garnish

Cut the chicken flesh from the bone and chop into small pieces so that they
may be conveniently wrapped in greaseproof paper, cut into 13-cm/5-inch
squares. Reserve the carcass for making stock or soup. Marinate the chicken
pieces in the soy sauce, sherry, sugar, ginger and monosodium glutamate
for 3 hours. The chicken pieces should then be individually wrapped,
envelope fashion, in the greaseproof paper, leaving a long 'tongue' that may
be adequately tucked in. Heat the oil to 180°C, 350°F, or until a day-old
cube of bread turns golden in 1 minute and deep-fry the 'packages' for
not more than 4-5 minutes; otherwise the paper will burn and the appearance will be spoiled.

  The cooked 'packages' should be laid out on a heated plate, one leaning
on another. For decoration, the 'packages' may be garnished with green
vegetables, such as broccoli, lettuce, watercress or a combination of
vegetables. Each diner should open a 'package' on a small plate in front of
him.

NOTE   Although the authentic recipe provides for only chicken meat to
be wrapped in the 'packages', there is no reason why other easily cooked
ingredients could not also be wrapped inside, for example, turkey, duck,
small pieces of pork or slices of steak.

Cantonese crystal chicken

Shui Ching Leng Keng Chi

Jellied meat (or meat and fish in aspic) appears more frequently in Chinese home cooking than in the West. In Canton, a version of steamed chicken with clear sauce has chrysanthemums round it and is called South-of-the-River one hundred flower chicken.

Serve for a family meal or party

METRIC/IMPERIAL	AMERICAN
1 (900-g-1·5-kg/2-3-lb) chicken	1 (2-3-lb) chicken)
4 thin slices cooked smoked ham	4 thin slices cooked smoked ham
1 teaspoon salt	1 teaspoon salt
1 teaspoon monosodium glutamate (optional)	1 teaspoon monosodium glutamate (optional)
3 tablespoons dry sherry	$\frac{1}{4}$ cup dry sherry
20 g/$\frac{3}{4}$ oz powdered gelatine	1$\frac{1}{2}$ envelopes powdered gelatin
900 ml/1$\frac{1}{2}$ pints superior broth (see page 170)	3$\frac{3}{4}$ cups superior broth (see page 170)

Clean the chicken thoroughly and dry. Place the chicken in a saucepan, cover with water, bring to the boil and simmer for 1 hour. Drain and when cool, chop the chicken into 24 pieces. Cut the ham into similar-sized pieces. Arrange the pieces of chicken and ham, interlaced in roof-tile fashion, in an oval dish.

Add the salt, monosodium glutamate, sherry and gelatine to the broth. Heat the broth mixture in a pan, stirring until the gelatine has melted and the ingredients are well mixed. Cool for 15 minutes and then pour over the chicken. Place the dish in the refrigerator for 2 hours. After 2 hours, the jellied chicken and ham should have set. Turn it out on to a plate.

NOTE   Arrange some colourful vegetable or fruit, such as finely-cut strips of sweet red and green peppers or strawberries, around the jellied food.

Onion-simmered duck

Ts'ung Yu Chia Hsiang

*What may seem unusual to the westerner about this recipe is the use of
pork as a stuffing. The meaty richness of the dish is counterbalanced,
however, by the spring greens or cabbage and the quantity of onions used.*

Serve for a family meal

METRIC/IMPERIAL	AMERICAN
2 onions	2 onions
100 g/4 oz roast pork	$\frac{1}{4}$ lb roast pork
100 g/4 oz dried Chinese mushrooms, soaked and drained	4 cups dried Chinese mushrooms, soaked and drained
1 teaspoon salt	1 teaspoon salt
1 tablespoon vegetable oil	1 tablespoon vegetable oil
1 (900-g-1·25-kg/2-2$\frac{1}{2}$-lb) duck	1 (2-2$\frac{1}{2}$-lb) duck
1 tablespoon light-coloured soy sauce	1 tablespoon light-colored soy sauce
2 hearts of spring greens or cabbage	2 spring lettuce or cabbage hearts
vegetable oil for deep-frying	vegetable oil for deep-frying
300 ml/$\frac{1}{2}$ pint superior broth (see page 170)	1$\frac{1}{4}$ cups superior broth (see page 170)
$\frac{1}{2}$ teaspoon monosodium glutamate (optional)	$\frac{1}{2}$ teaspoon monosodium glutamate (optional)
$\frac{1}{2}$ tablespoon oyster sauce (see page 161)	1$\frac{1}{2}$ teaspoons oyster sauce (see page 161)

Cut each onion into six sections. Slice the roast meat (across meat and fat)
into 0·5 × 2·5-cm/$\frac{1}{4}$ × 1-inch strips. Remove and discard the stalks from the
soaked mushrooms. Sprinkle the mushroom caps with half the salt and
sauté in the oil for 2 minutes. Combine these ingredients to make a stuffing.
Rub the skin of the duck with soy sauce and stuff with the mixture. Cut
the spring greens vertically through the middle into quarters.

Heat the oil to 180°C, 350°F, or until a day-old cube of bread turns golden
in 1 minute and deep-fry the duck for 1 minute. Drain. Place the duck in
a double-boiler (or deep casserole-type ovenproof dish, placed inside a
saucepan with water halfway up the dish). Pour the broth over the duck and
add the remaining salt, the monosodium glutamate and oyster sauce.
Simmer for 1 hour. Lift out the duck and line the dish with the leaves of
the spring green hearts. Replace the duck in the centre of the dish and simmer
for a further 30 minutes.

The duck may be served either in the casserole in which it was cooked or
in a large tureen. As this dish is extremely rich, it is best eaten with a large
quantity of rice.

Chinese ravioli
with prawn-pork filling

(Illustrated on page 125)

Hsien Hsia Chiao Tzu

This is one of the popular Chinese 'small-eat' items, or tea-house snacks, eaten between main meals. The filling may be made from vegetables, meats and seafoods. The Cantonese are very fond of seafood and this is their favourite version.

Serve as a snack

METRIC/IMPERIAL	AMERICAN
Chinese swallow-skin ravioli	*Chinese swallow-skin ravioli*
225 g/8 oz plain flour	2 cups all-purpose flour
$\frac{1}{4}$ teaspoon salt	$\frac{1}{4}$ teaspoon salt
900 ml/1$\frac{1}{2}$ pints boiling water	3$\frac{3}{4}$ cups boiling water
15 g/$\frac{1}{2}$ oz lard	1 tablespoon lard
Filling	*Filling*
225 g/8 oz cooked peeled prawns	$\frac{1}{2}$ lb cooked shelled shrimp
25 g/1 oz fat pork	2 tablespoons fatty pork
50 g/2 oz lean pork	$\frac{1}{4}$ cup lean pork
100 g/4 oz bamboo shoots	1 cup bamboo shoots
1 teaspoon salt	1 teaspoon salt
$\frac{1}{2}$ tablespoon soy sauce	1$\frac{1}{2}$ teaspoons soy sauce
1 tablespoon dry sherry	1 tablespoon dry sherry
$\frac{1}{2}$ teaspoon dry mustard	$\frac{1}{2}$ teaspoon dry mustard
$\frac{1}{2}$ tablespoon sesame oil	1$\frac{1}{2}$ teaspoons sesame oil
1 teaspoon castor sugar	1 teaspoon sugar
freshly ground black pepper	freshly ground black pepper

To make the *swallow-skin* dough, sift the flour into a bowl. Add the salt to the boiling water and pour into the flour. Stir quickly with a wooden spoon. Add the lard and knead well on a board. Divide the dough into 24 pieces and form each piece into a ball and roll out to circles 5-7·5 cm/ 2-3 inches in diameter.

For the filling, finely chop the prawns. Boil the lean and fat pork in water to cover for 5 minutes; then mince it finely. Cut the bamboo shoots into matchstick-thin strips and add to the prawns and pork in a bowl. Add the salt, soy sauce, sherry, mustard, oil, sugar and pepper to taste. Place in the refrigerator for 30 minutes.

Divide the filling into 24 portions. Place a little filling in the middle of each circle and fold both sides over the filling so they meet. Pinch the round sides together in the shape of a cock's comb. Place the 24 pieces on a greased ovenproof plate in a steamer. Cover and steam for 7 minutes. Serve immediately. Mix equal portions of vinegar and soy sauce and serve as a dip.

Cantonese chicken, ham and liver ensemble

(Illustrated on pages 146-147)

Kuangchow Wen-Chang Chi

This is an extremely attractive dish with the contrasting colours and textures of the three meats and the green vegetables.

Serve for a banquet

METRIC/IMPERIAL	AMERICAN
100 g/4 oz sliced cooked smoked ham	¼ lb sliced cooked smoked ham
675 g/1½ lb spring greens	1½ lb spring lettuce or cabbage
600 ml/1 pint superior broth (see page 170)	2½ cups superior broth (see page 170)
1 (1·5-kg/3-lb) chicken or chicken pieces	1 (3-lb) chicken or chicken pieces
100 g/4 oz chicken livers	¼ lb chicken livers
450 ml/¾ pint secondary broth (see page 163)	2 cups secondary broth (see page 163)
1 teaspoon salt	1 teaspoon salt
1 teaspoon castor sugar	1 teaspoon sugar
½ teaspoon monosodium glutamate (optional)	½ teaspoon monosodium glutamate (optional)
1 tablespoon cornflour	1 tablespoon cornstarch
1 tablespoon water	1 tablespoon water
1 teaspoon lard	1 teaspoon lard

Cut the ham into twenty-four 2·5 × 5-cm/1 × 2-inch thin pieces. Remove and discard the outer leaves of the spring greens, leaving only the hearts and tender leaves. Wash these and cut them into 18 pieces.

Bring the superior broth to the boil in a saucepan. Lower the chicken and livers into it. When the broth reboils, remove from the heat and cool for 30 minutes.

Take the chicken out of the broth, cut the meat from the bone and carve it into 24 slices. Cut the livers similarly. Reserve the broth. Cook the spring greens in boiling water for 5 minutes. Drain, add the secondary broth and three-quarters of the salt. Boil for another 5 minutes.

Arrange the ham, chicken and livers in three rows down the middle of an oval serving plate. Arrange the vegetables round them. Place the plate in a steamer and steam for 5 minutes.

Meanwhile, make a sauce by measuring 3 tablespoons (U.S. ¼ cup) of the reserved superior broth into a pan. Add the sugar, remaining salt and monosodium glutamate, the cornflour blended with the water, and the lard. Heat for 1 minute. Remove the plate from the steamer. Pour the sauce over the chicken before serving.

Cantonese fried noodles

(Illustrated on pages 146–147)

Kwangtung Chow Mein

This dish is usually eaten as a snack. It is placed in the centre of the table and divided into equal portions for the four, five or six people, as the case may be.

Serve as a snack

METRIC/IMPERIAL	AMERICAN
675 g/1½ lb lean beef steak or pork	1½ lb lean beef steak or pork
50 g/2 oz bamboo shoots	½ cup bamboo shoots
2 leeks	2 leeks
50 g/2 oz dried Chinese mushrooms, soaked and drained	2 cups dried Chinese mushrooms, soaked and drained
100 g/4 oz Chinese cabbage	¼ lb Chinese cabbage
3 tablespoon vegetable oil	¼ cup vegetable oil
450 g/1 lb cooked Chinese or egg noodles	1 lb cooked fine egg noodles
15 g/½ oz lard	1 tablespoon lard
1 tablespoon soy sauce	1 tablespoon soy sauce
salt and freshly ground black pepper	salt and freshly ground black pepper
1 tablespoon cornflour	1 tablespoon cornstarch
2 tablespoons water	3 tablespoons water
2 tablespoons chicken broth	3 tablespoons chicken broth
1 tablespoon white wine	1 tablespoon white wine
1 teaspoon sesame oil	1 teaspoon sesame oil
¼ teaspoon monosodium glutamate (optional)	¼ teaspoon monosodium glutamate (optional)
1 teaspoon castor sugar	1 teaspoon sugar

Slice the beef or pork, bamboo shoots, leeks and mushrooms into matchstick-thin strips. Cut the cabbage into 2·5-cm/1-inch pieces.

Heat half the oil in a large frying pan and sauté the noodles. After turning them over a few times, press the noodles evenly against the bottom of the pan with a wooden spoon until they form a flat, well spread-out cake. Cook over medium heat until the noodles at the bottom have become crispy—about 4 minutes. Turn the noodles over in one toss, like flipping a pancake. Sauté for a further 3 minutes, then transfer to a heated plate. Keep warm.

Heat the lard in the frying pan. Add the leeks, then the meat strips and stir-fry for 10-15 seconds. Add half the soy sauce and then the bamboo shoots and mushrooms. Sprinkle with pepper to taste. Stir-fry for 1 minute. Transfer the meat mixture to a plate and set aside.

Sprinkle the cabbage with salt, sauté in the remaining oil for 1 minute. Add the meat mixture to the cabbage and sauté for 30 seconds.

Meanwhile, blend the cornflour with the water. Add the remaining soy sauce, the broth, white wine, sesame oil, monosodium glutamate and sugar. Mix well and pour into the pan. After 15 seconds, lift out the meat mixture, place over the noodles and pour over the sauce from the pan.

Southwest China

This region of China has sometimes been referred to as the Great Southwest. Although it is a much smaller region than either the Northeast (Manchuria) or the Northwest (Sinkiang), it is composed of the three provinces of Yunnan, Kweichow and Kwangsi, with an area of approximately 270,000 square miles and a population of over 40 million. Isolated from the mainstream of events during the past half century, it was, in a way, 'rediscovered' by the people of the East Coast during the War of Resistance against Japan, when a great many enterprises, government offices and educational institutions had to move westwards. The communication between the East Coast and this area was so poor that those who moved to the back provinces of China, had either to travel hundreds of miles on foot or go by sea to Haiphong and Hanoi and come back into China again via the Hanoi-Yunnanfu railway.

The Great Southwest is the one area of China where the mountain ranges and rivers (and there are some great ones, such as the Mekong – called in Chinese the Gold Sand River) run north-south rather than east-west. Until recently, it was a feudal area, in spite of over 30 years of the Chinese Republican rule. The lords and ladies, or rather the warlords and their concubines, ate very well and their tables, like Henry VIII's high table, offered *haute cuisine* of sorts. The cooking of this area originates from these feudal 'high tables' and uses a wide choice of local produce, both vegetable and animal. The inland lakes of Tien and Erhhai or 'Ear Lake' are 5,000 feet above sea level and produce many types of freshwater fish, thus affording a variety of dishes.

Geographically, the region is beautiful. In Kwangsi, there are numerous hills and mountains which rise perpendicularly like stalagmites. Kunming, the capital of Yunnan, has the reputation of enjoying the best weather in China. In Kweichow, which is the nearest of the three to the Central Provinces, the cooking is motivated by the Mid-Yangtze and Szechwan cuisine. Being an extremely poor area, its cooking is largely compounded of its own home-cooking and these outside influences. Kwangsi, although fiercely independent, is very much inspired by its twin province, Kwantung, which is both richer and more populous and also the originator of the enormous Cantonese cuisine.

In these back provinces of China, much of the local produce and distinctive ingredients are uncommon plants and animals rarely seen or heard of anywhere else – bear's paws and sparrows are quite common delicacies. In my selection of recipes, I have had to confine myself to those ingredients that are generally available in a western kitchen.

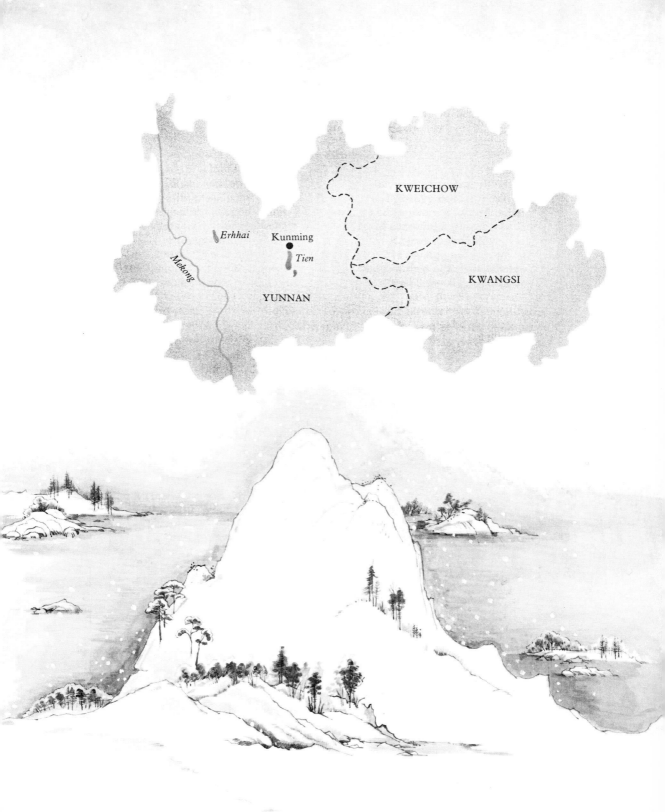

The Yunnan multi-dish snack

(Illustrated on page 165)

Kuo' Ch'iao Mi Chien

This tea-house food is usually prepared for one customer at a time.
However, quantities given here are sufficient for four.

Serve as a snack

METRIC/IMPERIAL	AMERICAN
1·4 litres/2½ pints duck or chicken broth	6 cups duck or chicken broth
½ teaspoon salt	½ teaspoon salt
¼ teaspoon monosodium glutamate (optional)	¼ teaspoon monosodium glutamate (optional)
freshly ground black pepper	freshly ground black pepper
100 g/4 oz breast of chicken	¼ lb chicken breast
100 g/4 oz pork fillet	¼ lb pork tenderloin
1 (100-g/4-oz) piece fish (sole, bass, salmon, carp or haddock)	1 (¼-lb) piece fish (sole, bass, salmon, carp or haddock)
100 g/4 oz pig's liver	¼ lb pork liver
100 g/4 oz pig's kidney	¼ lb pork kidney
100 g/4 oz Chinese celery cabbage	3 cups Chinese celery cabbage
100 g/4 oz leaf spinach	¼ lb leaf spinach
100 g/4 oz bean sprouts	1⅓ cups bean sprouts
75 g/3 oz egg noodles (or rice noodles)	1 cup egg noodles (or rice noodles)

By the time the broth is ready to be served, at least 2 tablespoons duck or chicken fat should be left in, which will help it to retain heat at the table. Add the salt, monosodium glutamate and pepper to taste. Slice the chicken, pork and fish into 2·5 × 5-cm/1 × 2-inch paper-thin strips. Dip the liver and kidney in boiling water for 1 minute and drain. Slice into paper-thin strips. Arrange the meats and fish on a small dish.

Cut the vegetables into pieces 2·5 cm/1 inch long. Plunge one vegetable at a time into boiling water for 1 minute and cool in fresh water for 3 minutes. Drain and arrange by colour on a separate dish. Boil the noodles for 5-6 minutes, drain and place on a third dish.

With the dishes of food, an adequate range of dips should also be provided, such as soy sauce, vinegar, Haisein sauce (see page 160), sesame oil and a mixture of salt and pepper. Heat one-third of the broth to boiling. Reserve the rest. Pour the hot broth into a tureen or ovenproof casserole and bring to the table. The diner eats the meats first. Using chopsticks, he submerges the pieces which require longer heating. The pieces which require less cooking, he merely dips into the soup for about 1 minute and then into one of the dips. After the meats have been eaten, the different vegetables are added to the broth, together with the remaining freshly-boiled broth. After half the vegetables have been consumed in the same fashion as the meats, the noodles are poured into the broth; a substantial soup.

Spinach balls

(Illustrated on page 145)

Po T'sai Yuan Tzu

These spinach balls have a heart of meat. They are made from ingredients obtainable almost everywhere and make a useful and interesting dish with multi-coloured appeal.

Serve for a family party

METRIC/IMPERIAL	AMERICAN
100 g/4 oz fat pork	$\frac{1}{4}$ lb fat back
225 g/8 oz lean pork	$\frac{1}{2}$ lb lean pork
2 eggs	2 eggs
1 teaspoon chopped fresh root ginger	1 teaspoon chopped fresh ginger root
1½ tablespoons chopped onion	2 tablespoons chopped onion
2 tablespoons boiling water	3 tablespoons boiling water
1 tablespoon cornflour	1 tablespoon cornstarch
$\frac{1}{2}$ teaspoon monosodium glutamate (optional)	$\frac{1}{2}$ teaspoon monosodium glutamate (optional)
1 teaspoon salt	1 teaspoon salt
freshly ground black pepper	freshly ground black pepper
900 g/2 lb fresh spinach	2 lb fresh spinach
25 g/1 oz dried Chinese mushrooms, soaked and drained	1 cup dried Chinese mushrooms, soaked and drained
50 g/2 oz bamboo shoots	$\frac{1}{2}$ cup bamboo shoots
25 g/1 oz cooked smoked ham	1 slice cooked smoked ham
300 ml/$\frac{1}{2}$ pint superior broth (see page 170)	1¼ cups superior broth (see page 170)
1 teaspoon sesame oil	1 teaspoon sesame oil

Finely mince the fat and lean pork and mix together in a bowl. Beat the eggs for 1 minute, then mix well into the pork. Infuse the ginger and onion in the boiling water for 6 minutes. Strain, discard the ginger and onion and pour the water into the pork mixture. Add the cornflour, half the monosodium glutamate, half the salt and pepper to taste. Beat the mixture thoroughly. Form into small meatballs.

Wash the spinach, remove the stalks and add to a large pan of boiling water for 10 seconds. Drain well and slice into matchstick-thin strips. Slice the mushrooms, bamboo shoots and ham into similar-sized strips. Mix together and spread on a tray. Roll the meatballs over this mixture to pick up the various coloured strips. Place them on an ovenproof plate. Cover and steam for 8 minutes.

Arrange any remaining spinach, mushrooms, bamboo shoots and ham in the bottom of a heated deep ovenproof dish. Place the meatballs on top. Meanwhile, make a sauce with the broth by adding the remaining monosodium glutamate and the remaining salt and pepper to taste. Heat and pour over the meatballs. Sprinkle with sesame oil and serve.

Salt and sour fish

(Illustrated opposite)

Yen Suan Yü

Chinese sweet and sour dishes are quite well known in the West, but it is not often that one comes across salt and sour dishes. In Kweichow, they have evolved a special ingredient for making this salt and sour pickle (see page 160). Fish cooked in this manner has a recognisable Kweichow flavour.

Serve for a family meal

METRIC/IMPERIAL	AMERICAN
1 (900-g-1·5-kg/2-3-lb) fish (carp, bass or mullet)	1 (2-3-lb) fish (carp, bass or mullet)
1 teaspoon salt	1 teaspoon salt
4 tablespoons salt and sour pickle (see page 160)	$\frac{1}{3}$ cup salt and sour pickle (see page 160)
1 clove garlic	1 clove garlic
1 medium onion	1 medium onion
3 slices fresh root ginger	3 slices fresh ginger root
1 tablespoon soy sauce	1 tablespoon soy sauce
1 tablespoon dry sherry	1 tablespoon dry sherry
2 teaspoons castor sugar	2 teaspoons sugar
25 g/1 oz lard	2 tablespoons lard
300 ml/$\frac{1}{2}$ pint water	1$\frac{1}{4}$ cups water
1 sweet red pepper	1 sweet red pepper
freshly ground black pepper	freshly ground black pepper
1 teaspoon monosodium glutamate (optional)	1 teaspoon monosodium glutamate (optional)
1$\frac{1}{2}$ teaspoons sesame oil	1$\frac{1}{2}$ teaspoons sesame oil
1 tablespoon cornflour	1 tablespoon cornstarch

Clean the fish, rub with the salt both inside and out and let stand for 1 hour. Chop the salt and sour pickle, garlic and onion and combine with the ginger, soy sauce, sherry and sugar.

Heat the lard in a fish kettle. Add the salt and sour mixture and stir-fry over high heat for 30 seconds. Add the water and bring to the boil, stirring.

Lower the fish into the boiling sauce, simmer for 10 minutes, turning the fish over once and basting all the time. Meanwhile, cut the pepper into thin strips. Carefully lift out the fish on to an oval heated serving dish. Add pepper to taste, monosodium glutamate and sesame oil to the sauce. Pour in the cornflour blended with a little water. Stir and, as soon as the sauce thickens, pour it over the fish. Serve immediately, garnished with the strips of red pepper.

Right *Spinach balls (see page 143); Salt and sour fish (see above).*
Overleaf *Paper-wrapped chicken (see page 134); Cantonese chicken, ham and liver ensemble (see page 138); Cantonese fried noodles (see page 139).*

Pot-steamed chicken

(Illustrated opposite)

Ch'i Kuo Chi

This is a famous Yunnan dish which is well-known throughout China. The basic method of cooking is steaming, which is generally recognised in China as a purist method.

Serve for a banquet or family meal

METRIC/IMPERIAL	AMERICAN
1 (1·5-1·75-kg/3-4-lb) chicken	1 (3-4-lb) chicken
2 slices fresh root ginger	2 slices fresh ginger root
2 teaspoons salt	2 teaspoons salt
freshly ground black pepper	freshly ground black pepper
1 teaspoon monosodium glutamate	1 teaspoon monosodium glutamate
(optional)	(optional)

Clean the chicken and chop (including bones) into about 24 pieces. Place the neck and bonier parts of the chicken around the bottom of a casserole or an authentic steam pot if you have one (see note). Build up layers, piece by piece, with the meatier portions until you reach the top layer, which should be slices of the chicken breast. Place the ginger slices over the chicken. Sprinkle with half the salt and put on the lid. Cover and steam (see note) for $3\frac{1}{2}$-4 hours.

When the steaming is complete, remove the lid and sprinkle the chicken with the remaining salt, pepper to taste and the monosodium glutamate. The steam pot, which is often a decorative piece of pottery, should be brought to the table and the lid opened ceremoniously in front of the diners.

NOTE   If the authentic Chinese pot for steam-distilling is unobtainable, invert an ovenproof plate inside a large saucepan. Fill the pan with 3 cm/ $1\frac{1}{2}$ inches of water. It is important for the plate to be about the same diameter as the bottom of the casserole so that the latter can sit comfortably on it, cushioned by a damp cloth. Place a heavy lid, preferably with a knob, upside down on top of the casserole. Place the casserole inside the saucepan on top of the inverted plate. Bring the water to the boil and steam. When the rising steam hits the inverted lid, some of it will condense, flow down the surface of the lid, and drip down the knob on to the chicken – a process which is very similar to what actually happens in the authentic Chinese steam pot. If too much water collects in the chicken, lower the heat.

Left *Pot-steamed chicken (see above).*

Chinese Moslem Cooking

Chinese Moslem cooking is one of the most widespread and best established styles of cooking in China. Although the Mohammedan Chinese live mostly in Sinkiang, the vast northwestern province, they are scattered throughout the whole of the Great Northwest, which includes such provinces as Tsinghai, Ningshia, Kansu, Shenshi and Inner Mongolia. There are many points of similarity between Chinese Moslem and Israeli cooking; both are widespread and derived their original inspiration from the deserts. Pork, the principal meat of China, rarely appears in either (although the Chinese Moslems do sometimes use it); and they are more inclined to use fish with scales rather than other forms of seafood. The whole of northwest China, largely an arid country, has traditionally been so poor that its inhabitants, many of whom are nomads, existed barely above subsistence level. Probably because of this bedouin desert background, their cooking is the direct opposite of Cantonese cooking which is full of sauces, delicacies and elaborate dishes. It might perhaps be that the whole strength and appeal of Chinese Moslem cooking is founded on its robust simplicity as opposed to the general sophistication of Chinese cooking at large.

The methods employed by the Chinese Moslems are basic: boiling (clear-simmering), barbecuing or roasting. The Chinese words for this type of cooking are *Ching Tseng* or clear and unadulterated.

In Peking, Moslem cooking constitutes one of the three main inspirations of Peking cuisine, and has a far greater influence on the capital's culinary repertoire than, say, Cantonese cooking. Such dishes as Mongolian barbecue (beef and lamb) and Peking duck (roasted by hanging in the oven) have come from the great Central Asian background of Chinese Moslem cooking.

This style of cooking is well advanced in the technique of using earthen pots. In fact, there are some Chinese restaurants (such as the Sa Kuo Chu of Peking, or 'Home of the Earthen Pot') that cook only in earthen pots, resulting in slow clear-simmering, rather than thick-stewing. The aim is to subject ingredients to prolonged, undisturbed cooking, so that eventually they can be presented in a soup of dew-like purity.

When a form of cooking specialises in beef and lamb, it is bound to find itself confined, unless it can make the best of all the bits and pieces of the animal – especially in an infertile land where economy is paramount. Chinese Moslem cooking has, therefore, developed a considerable expertise in the use of tails, brains, feet, liver and kidney. Indeed, this is an essential part of the delicacy of Chinese Moslem cooking.

SINKIANG

KANSU

INNER MONGOLIA

NINGSHIA

TSINGHAI

SHENSHI

Quick-fried sliced steak

(Illustrated on pages 166-167)

Ho Chien Pao Jou

This is a very quick and easy way of preparing a tender cut of beef.

Serve for a banquet or family meal

METRIC/IMPERIAL	AMERICAN
1 (350-g/12-oz) fillet of beef	1 ($\frac{3}{4}$-lb) piece beef tenderloin
2 tablespoons soy sauce	3 tablespoons soy sauce
1 tablespoon cornflour	1 tablespoon cornstarch
4 spring onions	4 scallions
300 ml/$\frac{1}{2}$ pint sesame oil	1$\frac{1}{4}$ cups sesame oil
1 clove garlic, crushed	1 clove garlic, crushed
1 tablespoon dry sherry	1 tablespoon dry sherry
1 tablespoon water	1 tablespoon water
1$\frac{1}{2}$ teaspoons vinegar	1$\frac{1}{2}$ teaspoons vinegar

Carve the meat across the grain into 3×2-cm/$1\frac{1}{2} \times \frac{3}{4}$-inch slices. Place in a bowl and add half the soy sauce and the cornflour. Mix well. Cut the spring onions into 1-cm/$\frac{1}{2}$-inch segments.

Heat the oil in a frying pan. Add the beef and gently stir-fry for 30 seconds. Drain and reserve the meat and the oil. Return the pan to the heat and add 1 tablespoon of the reserved oil, the garlic and spring onions. Stir-fry over high heat until the spring onions are well browned. Add the beef, sherry, remaining soy sauce, water and vinegar. Stir-fry quickly for 30 seconds and serve immediately.

Long-simmered beef

(Illustrated on page 168)

Wei Niu Jou

The beef in this dish is fried, boiled and then simmered with flavouring until it is almost a savoury jelly.

Serve for a family meal or party

METRIC/IMPERIAL	AMERICAN
1 (2·25-kg/5-lb) shin of beef	1 (5-lb) piece beef shank
4 tablespoons vegetable oil	$\frac{1}{3}$ cup vegetable oil
2 tablespoons castor sugar	3 tablespoons sugar
3 tablespoons soy sauce	$\frac{1}{4}$ cup soy sauce
4 tablespoons dry sherry	$\frac{1}{3}$ cup dry sherry
1 tablespoon dried tangerine	1 tablespoon dried tangerine
or orange peel, soaked and drained	or orange peel, soaked and drained
(see page 159)	(see page 159)
3 tablespoons finely chopped	$\frac{1}{4}$ cup finely chopped onion,
onion, or 6 spring onions	or 6 scallions
2 teaspoons chopped fresh	2 teaspoons chopped fresh
root ginger	ginger root

Trim the beef and cut into 2·5-cm/1-inch cubes. Stir-fry in the oil for 4 to 5 minutes over medium heat. Drain the meat, add to a pan of boiling water and boil for 3 minutes. Remove the meat and drain.

Place the beef in a heavy saucepan and barely cover with fresh cold water. Add the sugar, soy sauce, dry sherry, tangerine peel, onion and ginger. Lower the heat as far as possible and simmer, tightly covered, for 4 hours. Stir the contents of the pan once each hour. Transfer to a heated dish before serving.

Crisp-fried beef fritters

(Illustrated on pages 166-167)

Cha Niu Li Chi

These crisply fried beef fritters are dipped in salt and freshly ground black pepper before eating. Removing the pan from the heat prevents the food from burning while achieving maximum crispiness.

Serve for a banquet

METRIC/IMPERIAL	AMERICAN
1 (225-g/8-oz) fillet of beef	1 ($\frac{1}{2}$-lb) piece beef tenderloin
1 tablespoon chopped onion	1 tablespoon chopped onion
1 tablespoon chopped fresh root ginger	1 tablespoon chopped fresh ginger root
$\frac{1}{2}$ teaspoon monosodium glutamate (optional)	$\frac{1}{2}$ teaspoon monosodium glutamate (optional)
1 tablespoon sweet sherry	1 tablespoon sweet sherry
1 tablespoon sesame oil	1 tablespoon sesame oil
1 egg	1 egg
30 g/1 oz plain flour	$\frac{1}{4}$ cup all-purpose flour
15 g/$\frac{1}{2}$ oz cornflour	2 tablespoons cornstarch
150 ml/$\frac{1}{4}$ pint vegetable oil	$\frac{2}{3}$ cup vegetable oil
1 teaspoon salt	1 teaspoon salt
1 teaspoon freshly ground black pepper	1 teaspoon freshly ground black pepper

Cut the beef across the grain into $1 \times 2 \cdot 5$-cm/$\frac{1}{2} \times 1$-inch slices. Place in a bowl and add the onion, ginger, monosodium glutamate, sherry and 2 teaspoons of the sesame oil. Mix well with the fingertips and set aside to marinate for 30 minutes. Break the egg into a bowl and add the flour and cornflour. Blend and pour the mixture over the beef. Mix well.

Heat the vegetable oil in a frying pan. When hot, add the beef, piece by piece, spreading them out. Stir-fry gently over high heat for 2 minutes.

Remove the frying pan from the heat for 1 minute, letting the beef simmer at the reduced heat. Replace the pan over high heat for 1 minute of gentle stir-frying. Once again remove the pan from the heat for 1 minute. Repeat this process once more. This method of intermittent frying prevents the oil overheating and yet at the same time ensures that the fritters will become very crisp.

After the third frying, drain the beef fritters and place them on a heated serving dish. Sprinkle with the remaining sesame oil. Mix the salt and pepper and divide between two small dishes or saucers to use as a dip.

Braised triple white

(Illustrated on pages 166-167)

P'a San Pai

In a multi-course Chinese dinner, a dish like this, which is light and pure in colour, taste and texture, introduces an essential variation in a long procession of dishes.

Serve for a banquet

METRIC/IMPERIAL	AMERICAN
1 (100-g/4-oz) breast of chicken	1 ($\frac{1}{4}$-lb) chicken breast
4-6 spears fresh asparagus	4-6 spears fresh asparagus
1 heart of Chinese celery cabbage	1 Chinese celery cabbage heart
40 g/1$\frac{1}{2}$ oz chicken fat	3 tablespoons chicken fat
1 small onion, sliced	1 small onion, sliced
3 slices fresh root ginger	3 slices fresh ginger root
150 ml/$\frac{1}{4}$ pint superior broth	$\frac{2}{3}$ cup superior broth
(see page 170)	(see page 170)
1 tablespoon dry sherry	1 tablespoon dry sherry
1 teaspoon salt	1 teaspoon salt
1 tablespoon cornflour	1 tablespoon cornstarch
1 teaspoon monosodium glutamate	1 teaspoon monosodium glutamate
(optional)	(optional)
6 tablespoons milk	$\frac{1}{2}$ cup milk

Cut the breast of chicken into 0·5 × 3-cm/$\frac{1}{4}$ × 1$\frac{1}{2}$-inch strips. Scrape the asparagus spears. Dip both the cabbage heart and asparagus spears in boiling water for 1 minute. Then cut the asparagus and shred the cabbage into 3-5-cm/1$\frac{1}{2}$-2-inch lengths.

Heat two-thirds of the chicken fat in a frying pan. Sauté the onion and ginger for 30 seconds. Add the broth and sherry. Bring to the boil, simmer for 1 minute and then discard the onion and ginger. Add the chicken, asparagus and cabbage to the pan by lowering each separately into the boiling broth. Sprinkle with salt and cook for 3 minutes.

Blend the cornflour, monosodium glutamate and milk, then mix with some of the hot broth and pour over the contents of the pan. Bring back to the boil, stirring continuously until lightly thickened. Slip the remaining chicken fat into the side of the pan and serve as soon as the fat has melted.

Glossary

Bamboo shoots

These are eaten probably more for their crunchy texture than for their taste, which is extremely subtle and verging on tastelessness. There is not a great deal of difference between ordinary bamboo shoots and winter bamboo shoots except that the latter are somewhat more tender and smaller and are used by the Chinese for special dishes. They are usually available canned, either whole or in large pieces. Rinse well with cold water before using. Bamboo shoots may be kept covered with water in a tightly sealed jar in the refrigerator for a week, if the water is changed every few days.

Bean-curd

Soy bean purée is set in cake form (about 7·5 cm/3 inches square and 2·5 cm/1 inch thick) to make bean-curd. It is an unusually soft, spongy custard, creamy in colour, highly nutritious and widely used in China. Its own flavour is slight, but it absorbs and complements that of other foods. Treated as a vegetable, it may be cooked with almost any meat, fish or vegetable. It may also be used in soups. Bean-curd is available either dried or fresh. The former does not require refrigeration if it is kept tightly wrapped and used within a few months. The latter may be kept covered with water in a tightly sealed jar in the refrigerator for a week, if the water is changed every few days.

Bean-curd cheese, red *(Chinese red cheese)*

This is a salty, very strong tasting substance which is a fermented derivative of bean-curd. It has no western equivalent in flavour. In China, it is served in various ways; by itself, in small quantities to accompany rice, or cooked together with meat, fish or vegetables. Mash the cubes before using. It may be bought canned in a red sauce. It can be kept in a covered jar in the refrigerator for several weeks.

Bean paste, red

This is a sweetened purée of red beans which is used for stuffing, steamed pastries and for other sweet dishes.

Bean sprouts

They are actually the sprouts or shoots of Mung peas which are tiny whitish-green shoots with a crunchy texture. Most Chinese restaurants grow their own – easily done in a few days by placing the Mung peas between pieces of clean damp cloth or blanket and keeping them at a constant, fairly warm temperature (preferably indoors). They should be cooked only briefly so that their crunchy quality is retained. Since they are so inexpensive, they are used extensively in all Chinese restaurants. They may be bought fresh, in cans or in packages.

Beans, fermented black *(black bean sauce)*

These small beans are preserved soy beans which are very salty. They have a strong flavour. If unavailable, add extra salt to the recipe. They may

156

be stored in a tightly sealed jar. These usually come dried and must be soaked and often mashed before using.

Beans, fermented brown *(brown bean sauce)*

This very thick and spicy paste, which is made from yellow beans, flour and salt, is fermented. The beans are cooked before using. It may be used as an alternative to fermented black beans for frying and cooking with meats. It is available in small jars or cans.

Bêche-de-mer *(sea cucumber)*

This is a species of jellyfish which is the same shape as a small, wrinkled cucumber. It is also occasionally used in French cooking. In China, it usually comes dried hard, greyish-black in colour, and 10-26 cm/4-10 inches long. Before using, scrub and soak for 24 hours in warm water, changing the water several times. Clean carefully, removing the internal organs, then rinse in fresh water. When soaked, it becomes a gelatinous mass with some fairly hard parts. It is usually cooked with poultry, meat or chicken broth. It is considered a delicacy and is probably eaten more for its texture and rarity than for its taste, which is subtle to the point of almost being tasteless. However, it enhances the flavour of other foods cooked with it.

Brown soy jam *(brown soy paste)*

This is used when a lighter coloured soy jam is needed. Basically, it is the same as soy jam except for the colour.

Cabbage

Chinese celery cabbage (Chinese lettuce): normally sold in shops as Chinese leaves. Crisp vegetable resembling Cos lettuce which has firm, tightly packed, vertical leaves that are pale yellow with a light green colour at the tips. As a substitute, use young celery, Swiss chard or Savoy cabbage.
Chinese cabbage (Chinese chard): an extremely versatile and popular vegetable that has long, smooth, whitish stems and large, dark green, crinkly leaves. It requires little cooking and has a delicate flavour.
Chinese salted cabbage: the cabbages that are usually salted are green, and are generally salted and dried in the sun. Sometimes hot pepper is added. Salted cabbage is used with meat as a flavouring agent. It must be soaked for 15 minutes in warm water, then rinsed in several changes of cold water.
Mustard cabbage: similar in taste to broccoli, this dark green vegetable has tightly packed scalloped leaves. It is similar in both size and texture to a small head of cabbage.

Chilli peppers

These are small, red peppers, usually no more than 5-7.5 cm/2-3 inches in length and shaped like an irregular horn. They are extremely hot in taste (probably the hottest vegetable in existence). The white seeds inside are usually discarded. Chilli peppers often come dried, in which case they are even hotter. They are often fried to impregnate oil with their hotness. This oil is then used to cook meats and vegetables. When dried chilli peppers are fried in oil, they give it a red colour; this oil is called *chilli oil* and is sometimes used – mixed with soy sauce – as a dip at the table. These peppers are naturally used very sparingly. They may be purchased loose. Green and yellow chilli peppers are occasionally available.

Chinese ham

The two best known hams in China are the *Yunnan ham* and the *Ching Hua ham*. They are usually available sliced in cans. A good substitute is the *Smithfield ham* – the redder the colour, the more similar it is to the Chinese variety.

Chinese noodles

These are similar to the Italian spaghetti and the thinner thread-like variety, vermicelli, except that Chinese noodles are usually finer and superior in quality. The Italian products make good substitutes, however. Chinese noodles come in four varieties:

Egg noodles: more yellow in colour than the following types, egg noodles are often precooked in 'pads' (like a small ball of wool but flattened). Precooked, they require only a short period of simmering in boiling water to loosen up before they are stir-fried, cooked in sauce or added to soups. Dried egg noodles may be stored in a closed plastic bag. Fresh egg noodles may be kept several weeks if tightly sealed in plastic bags and placed in the refrigerator.

Rice stick noodles (rice flour noodles): usually whiter in colour than the wheat flour noodles, these come in straight, fine strands, about 20 cm/8 inches in length. In the south, where they are more popular, they are often cooked with wood-ears, mushrooms, meats or various seafoods, such as oysters.

Transparent pea-starch noodles: although the noodles are somewhat white and opaque when raw, they become transparent after a period of soaking or simmering in water. The distinct advantage of this variety is that they do not become soft and mushy when cooked, yet are able to absorb an enormous amount of broth or gravy. Therefore, they are an excellent assembler of flavours. Unlike other noodles, they are never eaten on their own; they are always cooked with meat, gravy, soup or vegetables. Soak in warm water for a few minutes before using to prevent absorbing excessive liquid from the prepared dish. They are made from ground Mung peas. Vermicelli may be substituted.

Wheat flour noodles: these form the staple diet of the North Chinese. When Marco Polo brought them back to Europe in the late 13th century, they became known as spaghetti. These noodles look like spaghetti and are made largely from the same ingredients. When cooked, they should be soft outside but still firm inside. They should never be overcooked.

158

Doilies for Peking duck

makes about 20

Very similar in appearance to ordinary pancakes, these are made without eggs and heated without the use of fat. Very thin, ordinary pancakes may be substituted.

METRIC/IMPERIAL	AMERICAN
175 g/6 oz plain flour	1½ cups sifted all-purpose flour
150 ml/¼ pint boiling water	⅔ cup boiling water
3 tablespoons sesame oil	4 tablespoons sesame oil

Place the sifted flour in a bowl. Pour in the boiling water very slowly and gradually work to a warm dough. Knead gently for 1 to 2 minutes; then let stand for 10 minutes. Shape the dough into a roll 5 cm/2 inches in diameter. Cut the roll into 20 thin slices. Brush one side of each slice generously with sesame oil and lay another slice on top of it with the oiled surfaces together like a sandwich. Roll the double piece out from the centre on a lightly floured working surface until it spreads out to a pancake with a diameter of about 13 cm/5 inches. Make as many pancakes as the dough allows. Heat a large, flat, heavy, ungreased frying pan or omelette pan over low heat. When quite hot, place the pancake in the pan. Rotate the pan above the heat every so often so that the cooking is even. When the pancake starts to bubble, turn it over. After 2 or 3 minutes of heating on both sides, pull each double piece of dough apart into separate slices. Fold each piece into a half circle on the side brushed with sesame oil. Pile the doilies on a plate and place in a steamer for 10 minutes, steaming before bringing them to the table for wrapping around pieces of duck. In China, such doilies are simply termed 'thin cakes' (Po Bin).

Dried Chinese mushrooms

Fresh mushrooms are seldom used in Chinese cooking. The Chinese prefer the dried ones, which are brownish-black in colour and have a much stronger flavour and firmer texture than ordinary mushrooms. Clean them by rinsing in cold water, then soak in warm water for 20 to 30 minutes before use. The mushroom water itself makes an excellent flavouring agent. Soaked mushrooms may be kept several days if drained, then wrapped in aluminium foil and refrigerated.

Dried tangerine or orange peel *(Mandarin orange peel)*

The dried peel of citrus fruits has a stronger flavour than fresh peel; therefore, it is used only in small quantities. If commercially unavailable, prepare it by drying fresh peel in a very cool oven (120°C, 250°F, Gas Mark ½) for 3 hours. Turn the heat off and let stand in the oven overnight. Dried peel is usually soaked for 30 to 45 minutes before using.

Egg noodles *(see Chinese noodles)*

Fermented black beans *(see beans, fermented black)*

Five-spice powder

This very strong, fragrant, mixed spice powder consists of star aniseed, aniseed pepper, fennel, cloves and cinnamon. It is extremely pungent and should be used sparingly. Allspice may be used as a substitute.

Ginger, root

This root varies from 5 mm/$\frac{1}{4}$ inch to 2·5 cm/1 inch in diameter and 7·5-15 cm/3-6 inches in length. It has a coarse, yellow skin and is green inside with a white core. Scrape the root before using. Thin slices (about 3 mm/$\frac{1}{8}$ inch thick) are cut from the root as required. It is a very strong flavouring agent. The unused portion is wrapped in foil and can last for weeks or even months. Store in a cool, dry place, in the refrigerator or freeze without washing or scraping. Sliced fresh green ginger is also available in 125-g/$4\frac{1}{2}$-oz cans.

Ginger water

Prepare ginger water by placing 1 tablespoon chopped, fresh root ginger into a pan with 5 tablespoons (U.S. 6 tablespoons) water. Simmer over low heat for 3 minutes, strain and use as required.

Haisein sauce or Hoisin sauce *(red vegetable sauce)*

Very similar in appearance to plum sauce—thick and viscous, brownish-red in colour, with a pungent sweet spiciness about it—this sauce is made from soy beans, garlic, chilli, sugar and vinegar. Unlike plum sauce, it is used primarily in cooking, especially with shellfish, spare ribs, pork, duck, chicken and vegetables. It may be kept in a tightly sealed jar in the refrigerator for several months.

Kumquats

These are small mandarins which often grow on very decorative miniature potted trees. They are usually preserved in a syrup.

Kweichow salt and sour pickle

This salt and sour pickle can be used with either meat or fish dishes, and in small quantities with other vegetable dishes.

Makes 900 ml 1$\frac{1}{2}$ pints (U.S. 3$\frac{3}{4}$ cups)

METRIC/IMPERIAL	AMERICAN
3 hearts of spring greens	3 spring lettuce or cabbage hearts
6 cloves garlic	6 cloves garlic
3 teaspoons salt	3 teaspoons salt
2 tablespoons dry sherry	3 tablespoons dry sherry
2 tablespoons salt	3 tablespoons salt
2 tablespoons chilli powder	3 tablespoons chili powder
2 teaspoons castor sugar	2 teaspoons sugar
600 ml/1 pint sweet sherry	2$\frac{1}{2}$ cups sweet sherry

Chop the hearts of spring greens into 1-cm/$\frac{1}{2}$-inch pieces. Crush the garlic and mix with the chopped hearts. Place in a casserole. Cover and cook in a cool oven (150°C, 300°F, Gas Mark 2) for 30 minutes. Remove from the oven and let cool for 2 hours. Sprinkle with the 3 teaspoons salt. Pour the dry sherry over the mixture and mix well. Cover the casserole again and let the contents stand for 3 days at room temperature. After 3 days, mix in the 2 tablespoons (U.S. 3 tablespoons) salt, chilli powder, sugar and sweet sherry. Pour the mixture into a sterilized airtight jar and seal. Let the mixture stand for 50 days before using.

Leeks *(see spring onions and leeks)*

Lychee
Now becoming popular in the West, this fruit consists of a thin brittle shell enclosing a sweet, jelly-like pulp and a single seed. It is white and resembles a grape in texture. It is usually sold canned in a light syrup. Unused fruit may be placed in a tightly sealed jar and refrigerated.

Lotus leaves *(water lily leaves)*
The leaves of the lotus plant come in large sheets, often more than 46 cm/18 inches across. In Chinese cooking, they are frequently used for wrapping together various foods and flavouring ingredients before steaming them. In this way, the food absorbs the flavour of the leaf. Since lotus leaves are not easily obtainable in the West, a large cabbage leaf may be used as a substitute.

Lotus root *(water lily root)*
This reddish-brown tuberous stem is similar in texture to a potato but better tasting and less woody. Soak for 20 minutes in hot water, rinse, then peel before using.

Lotus seeds *(water lily seeds)*
These are oval and about 1 cm/½ inch long. They have a very delicate flavour. To prepare, pour over hot water and let stand for 5 minutes. Remove and discard the dark brown husk and the small germ portion of the seed which has a very bitter taste. Rinse in fresh water. Place in a pan, cover with water, boil 10 to 15 minutes. Drain and use as required. Blanched almonds may be substituted.

Monosodium glutamate
This is a white, powdery substance which, when added in small quantities, enhances or accentuates the taste of foods. When increasing quantities of a recipe, the amount of the monosodium glutamate should remain unaltered. It is used extensively in Japan and (more recently) in China. Chicken stock cubes, which often contain a proportion of the same substance, may be used as a substitute. One chicken stock cube is the equivalent of 1 teaspoon monosodium glutamate.

Oyster sauce
A thick, greyish-brown liquid, this concentrate of oysters, soy sauce and brine is usually sold in bottles or cans. It is used as a flavouring agent for cooking with meat, poultry and seafood. It does not require refrigeration.

Pickled vegetables

There is a wide range of pickled vegetables in China. The following are the most popular and easily available in the West.

Kweichow salt and sour pickle: making this pickled cabbage is usually a complicated procedure, but the recipe for a simplified version is given on page 160.

Pow Tsai: this is often made at home by bottling the chopped crunchy parts of white cabbage in brine, adding gin or whisky and dried chilli peppers.

Red in snow: this salty pickled vegetable is usually used for cooking with ground meats.

Szechwan cabbage (Tsa Tzai): hot and salty, this usually comes in small cans. It is used sliced or chopped for cooking in, and considerably increasing the flavour of the meats.

Plum sauce

This is a thick, amber-red sauce made traditionally from plums or apricots, sugar, chilli and vinegar. It is generally used as a table condiment for roast duck, pork and spare ribs. It is only occasionally used in cooking. If desired, a dash of sugar may be added if the sauce tastes too tart. It is available in jars and cans.

Plum sauce may be made at home using the following recipe.

Plum sauce

Makes 600 ml/1 pint (U.S. 2½ cups)

METRIC/IMPERIAL	AMERICAN
12 dark plums	12 dark plums
6 tablespoons water	½ cup water
3 tablespoons soy jam	¼ cup soy jam
1 tablespoon castor sugar	1 tablespoon sugar

Peel the plums, remove the stones and cut into quarters. Place in a saucepan with the water and simmer uncovered over low heat until very soft. Add the soy jam and the sugar. Stir and cook for a further 10 to 12 minutes, stirring continuously. Store in a covered jar in the refrigerator and use as required.

Pow Tsai *(see pickled vegetables)*

Red bean paste *(see bean paste, red)*

Red bean-curd cheese *(see bean-curd cheese, red)*

Red in snow *(see pickled vegetables)*

Rice stick noodles *(see Chinese noodles)*

Rock sugar, brown *(rock candy)*

The Chinese use large grains or lumps of crystallised sugar in cooking. Ordinary brown sugar may be substituted.

Salt and sour pickle *(see Kweichow salt and sour pickle)*

Secondary broth

Bones are the only ingredients used in the preparation of secondary broth; chicken bones, fresh pork bones and smoked pork bones in the ratio of 2:2:1. Place the bones in a large saucepan and cover with water three times the depth of the bones. Simmer for 4 hours, skimming at hourly intervals.

Sesame jam *(sesame paste)*

Made from ground sesame seeds, this tastes and looks like peanut butter. It is sometimes called *tahina* and may be purchased in some health food stores or stores specialising in Oriental foods. Sesame jam will keep for months if placed in a tightly covered jar and refrigerated. A good substitute may be obtained by adding a teaspoon of sesame oil to about $2-2\frac{1}{2}$ tablespoons of peanut butter.

Sesame oil

This is similar to corn oil, with a strong nutty taste and fragrance. Sesame oil is used sparingly as a flavouring agent (usually less than a teaspoon at a time). It is made from toasted sesame seeds.

Sesame paste *(see sesame jam)*

Soy herbal sauce *(master broth)*

This is an aromatic sauce used generously to cook plain, chunky, raw ingredients such as hard-boiled egg, whole chicken, duck, leg or shoulder of pork, kidney or chicken livers. It eliminates unacceptable flavours.

Soy herbal sauce

A dark sauce used extensively to add a savoury flavour.

Makes 1·75 litres/3 pints (U.S. 7½ cups)

METRIC/IMPERIAL	AMERICAN
1 bouquet garni	1 bouquet garni
1 teaspoon five-spice powder (see page 160)	1 teaspoon five-spice powder (see page 160)
1·75 litres/3 pints water	7½ cups water
150 ml/¼ pint soy sauce	⅔ cup soy sauce
scant ½ litre/¾ pint dry sherry	2 cups dry sherry
2 teaspoons salt	2 teaspoons salt
5 tablespoons brown sugar	6 tablespoons brown sugar
2 teaspoons monosodium glutamate	2 teaspoons monosodium glutamate
¼ teaspoon freshly ground black pepper	¼ teaspoon freshly ground black pepper
1½ tablespoons dried tangerine or orange peel (see page 159)	2 tablespoons dried tangerine or orange peel (see page 159)

Make a bouquet garni (3 bay leaves, 3 sprigs parsley and 1 sprig thyme tied together). Place with all the remaining ingredients in a large pot (preferably china or earthenware, protected from the heat by an asbestos mat) and simmer for 1 hour. Remove the bouquet garni. The resulting liquid is then ready and may be used repeatedly. It will keep indefinitely in the refrigerator. Each time it is used, the liquid is enriched further. It should be strained occasionally, and every third time it is used, a fresh bouquet garni should be added, and then removed before refrigerating.

Soy jam *(soy paste, soy-bean paste)*
This thick, viscous, almost black paste is made from fermented soy beans. It is similar in flavour, and therefore may be interchanged with soy sauce. Soy jam is usually used where a thicker sauce is required – in the quick-frying of diced meat, for example. It may be obtained in cans or jars.

Right *The Yunnan multi-dish snack (see page 142).*
Overleaf *Quick-fried sliced steak (see page 152); Crisp-fried beef fritters (see page 154); Braised triple white (see page 155).*

Soy sauce

This is a fermented sauce made from soy beans, wheat, yeast and salt. The sediment which forms is soy jam. Both the colour and thickness of the sauce may vary from light to dark and thick to thin. For small quantities, 1 teaspoon salt or 1 beef stock cube dissolved in a little hot water may be substituted for 2 tablespoons (U.S. 3 tablespoons) soy sauce.

Light-coloured soy sauce: very delicate and is used where flavour is desired without excessive colour.

Dark soy sauce: rich, full-bodied and has caramel added. Used where flavour and colour is desired.

Spring onions and leeks

The Chinese generally cook with the whole length of the spring onion cut into segments as required. The flavour is extracted by sautéing in oil or fat. Both the green tops and the white bulbs are used for garnishing dishes. Leeks are usually selected to cook with the stronger flavoured meats and with some varieties of fish.

Superior broth

This broth is essential in Chinese cooking and is usually produced in quantity in China by a fairly long and stylised process. The whole process may be shortened. A simplified recipe is on page 170. The broth will be only slightly different from the traditional Chinese superior broth. Canned chicken or beef consommé may be substituted.

Left *Long-simmered beef (see page 153).*

Superior broth

This is a simplified version of the traditional Chinese superior broth.

Makes 2·25 litres/4 pints (U.S. 10 cups)

METRIC/IMPERIAL	AMERICAN
1 (900-g/2-lb) chicken or chicken pieces	1 (2-lb) chicken or chicken pieces
1 (900-g/2-lb) shoulder of pork	1 (2-lb) pork shoulder
1 (900-g/2-lb) pork bone	1 (2-lb) pork bone
1 (450-g/1-lb) smoked pork or ham bone	1 (1-lb) smoked pork or ham bone
2·25 litres/4 pints water	10 cups water
1 tablespoon chopped onion	1 tablespoon chopped onion
1 teaspoon chopped fresh root ginger	1 teaspoon chopped fresh ginger root
1 tablespoon soy sauce	1 tablespoon soy sauce

Remove the breast meat and the drumsticks from the chicken. Boil the remainder with the shoulder of pork and bones in the water or water to cover for 15 minutes. Meanwhile, finely chop the meat from the chicken breast and drumsticks, keeping the light and dark meat separate, and set aside.

Skim the broth. Lift out the chicken, pork and bones. Place them in a bowl with 1·15 litres/2 pints (U.S. 5 cups) cold water. Pour half of this water into the broth. The coolness coagulates the grease and impurities, making them easier to remove. Skim. Pour a quarter of the broth into another bowl to cool. This cooling broth will be used as the bowl of cold water was used earlier. Return the chicken, pork and bones to the broth. Simmer the mixture for 1 hour. The simmering should now be gentle throughout the process. It is important not to allow the broth to reach a full boil at any time as this will create a 'stewed' instead of a 'clear' broth. After 1 hour, remove the chicken, pork and bones and place in the remaining cold water. Add the cooling broth to the pan, thus again coagulating more grease and impurities, which are once again removed. This process is repeated another two to three times until the broth becomes strong and pure.

In the final phase, add the onion, root ginger and soy sauce to the broth. The chopped chicken meats are used as the final clarifiers. The dark meat from the drumsticks is the first clarifier and the white meat is the second. In each case, the chopped chicken is simmered in the broth for about 10 minutes. Then the broth is strained through a sieve and the meat, onion and root ginger discarded. The broth will keep for 3 to 4 days in the refrigerator. For making larger quantities, a duck may be added for every two chickens, but only chicken meat should be used for clarifying.

Sweet dew sauce

This is a version of Haisein sauce. It is a sweet vegetable sauce which can be used for cooking or as a dip.

Sweetened soy jam
This is soy jam with sugar added.

Szechwan cabbage *(Tza Tsai) (see pickled vegetables)*

Transparent pea-starch noodles *(see Chinese noodles)*

Water chestnuts
A root vegetable, round and somewhat flat in shape, water chestnuts have sweet, sugary juice and a crunchy texture. Their taste and texture do not seem to alter when canned. This is the only form in which they are available in the West. Water chestnuts are commonly mixed with minced meats to add crunchiness. They may be kept covered with water in a tightly sealed jar in the refrigerator for a week if the water is changed every few days.

Wheat flour noodles *(see Chinese noodles)*

Wine-sediment paste
This is a thick paste, often maroon although it may be purple or cream coloured. It is made from wine sediment and fermented rice. Wine-sediment paste is used in cooking meats, poultry, seafood and especially snails. It has the effect of strengthening the taste of foods as well as surpassing a pronounced fish flavour. An acceptable substitute for it may be made by blending together in a liquidiser 1 tablespoon red bean-curd cheese, 1 large finely chopped onion, 1 teaspoon finely chopped root ginger, 2 teaspoons finely chopped tangerine or orange peel, 2 teaspoons brown sugar, 2 crushed cloves garlic, 3 tablespoons (U.S. $\frac{1}{4}$ cup) dry sherry, 1 tablespoon tomato purée, 1 teaspoon finely ground rice, 1 tablespoon brandy (optional), and 3 tablespoons (U.S. $\frac{1}{4}$ cup) red wine. Reduce the volume of the mixture by one-third to one-half by simmering over low heat in a large, shallow frying pan. The resulting paste should be red and thick.

Winter bamboo shoots *(see bamboo shoots)*

Winter melon
There are a great variety of melons in China. They are naturally rarer in winter than in summer. Just as the Chinese demand for winter bamboo shoots is an expression of Chinese finesse and perversity, so is the demand for winter melon. A young vegetable marrow or courgettes may be substituted.

Wood-ears
This is a species of lichen. The type often used in Chinese cooking is black in colour and dried. Before using the fungi, soak for about an hour and clean in several changes of water. Like bamboo shoots, they are used more for their texture (crunchy and slippery) than for their taste, which again is bland. The *Cloud-ear* is white and shaped like a cloud, as its name indicates. There is also *Silver-ear fungus* which are sometimes used in sweetened soups. Button mushrooms may be used as a substitute.

Chinese Cooking Methods

Deep-frying

Except in restaurants or food stalls, deep-frying in the western sense is very seldom seen in Chinese households. What the Chinese use in home cooking is a Chinese pan, known as a *wok*, which slopes towards the centre (thus creating a well of oil in the middle) holding $\frac{1}{4}$–$\frac{1}{2}$ pint (150-300 ml) of oil. A pair of bamboo chopsticks or a perforated spoon is used to turn the food over in the oil. The advantage of this Chinese pan is that when the food is pushed on to the sloping sides, the oil will start to drain towards the centre. In a western kitchen, where the pan is equipped with a wire basket, deep-frying is much simpler.

Static-frying

There are two main categories.

Chien: larger ingredients may be used than in the various categories of quick stir-frying, with only limited stirring movements. A typical example of Chien is in the static-frying of bread.

Tieh: different from *Chien* in that normally only one side of the food is cooked. The food is not turned over as with bread. It is, in fact, often the practice to sprinkle the top side of the food with water, vinegar, broth or a mixture of all three. Thus, the food produced will turn out soft on the top and crispy on the bottom. *Tieh* is also a term that sometimes indicates foods which are cooked in large chunks, or slices cooked on both sides. After the cooking is complete, the food is removed quickly from the pan and sliced into smaller pieces before serving.

Steaming

This method is used more frequently in Chinese cooking than in western cooking, probably because either boiling or steaming rice produces large quantities of steam. This steam is utilised to cook other dishes by placing layers of steamers (which are basket work trays) on top of the rice. Thus, when the rice is ready, a whole series of dishes will also be ready at the same time! Besides, all the dishes are kept very hot without the use of electric hot-plates or a bain-marie (hot water bath). If a steamer is not available, an ovenproof dish or plate may be inverted in a large saucepan. The food to be steamed should be placed in an ovenproof bowl and set on top of the inverted plate. Fill the saucepan until the bowl holding the food is one-third underwater. When the water boils, the steaming will start. In short-steaming, the bowl containing the food can be left open, as in the cooking of fish; in long-steaming (steaming over 30 minutes), the food is usually cooked covered. This can be done with a lid or by covering the top of the bowl with aluminium foil. The large saucepan should be covered tightly in both instances.

Quick stir-frying *(quick-frying)*

One of the most commonly employed and distinctive methods of Chinese cooking is the *Ch'ao* or quick-frying, or more graphically, quick-stir-frying. The process consists primarily of cooking one, or a number of foods, which are sliced into thin or matchstick-thin strips, in one or a few table-spoons of oil or fat. The ingredients in the pan are stirred with a metal spoon, spatula or a pair of bamboo chopsticks, while the ingredients cook. Seasonings and sauces are added and adjusted from time to time. Often the foods to be cooked together are stir-fried separately first, and then finally combined together in one big crescendo of cooking. This is sometimes necessary since the different foods combined in the dishes may require different lengths of cooking time. Another reason for separate cooking is the need to keep the flavours quite distinct, until the final assembly. As a rule, the oil used in quick-stir-frying is corn or peanut oil; however, chicken fat is often employed in delicate cooking, for instance, to sauté vegetables. For ordinary cooking, lard is employed.

There are three main categories of quick-stir-frying:

Ch'ao: the quick-stir-frying as described above.

Liu: indicates wet-frying. The process starts in the same way as in *Ch'ao* or *Pao,* but the stirring is less vigorous. The movements are aimed more at turning over the foods rather than scrambling them. After the first phase of the frying, a mixture consisting of cornflour, broth, sugar, vinegar and soy sauce is generally introduced. The sauce is usually prepared before-hand in a separate bowl and is added only 30 seconds to 1 minute before the cooking is completed. As soon as the sauce thickens, the dish is served.

Pao: also the Chinese word for explosion. In this type of stir-frying, the heat is turned to the highest setting, therefore the process must be short and sharp, usually lasting not much more than 1 minute, often much less. The food used in the cooking is usually marinated and often cooked on its own or combined with one or two others. In contrast, *Ch'ao* often has as many as half a dozen foods fried together.

Index